WADSWORTH PHILOSOPHERS SERIES

W9-AVS-657

ON

OCKHAM

Sharon M. Kaye
John Carroll University, Cleveland, Ohio

Robert M. Martin
Dalhousie University, Halifax, Nova Scotia

WADSWORTH

TM

THOMSON LEARNING

Australia • Canada • Mexico • Singapore • Spain
United Kingdom • United States

WADSWORTH

★ ™

THOMSON LEARNING

We are very grateful to many persons and institutions for helping to make this project possible. In particular, we would like to mention: John Carroll University, for granting Kaye's postdoctoral research leave and for providing a summer research grant; the I. W. Killam Trust, for funding Kaye's research fellowship; and Dalhousie University, for funding Martin's travel grant. Finally, we would like to thank each of our departments, as well as our family and friends, for their advice and encouragement.

Printed in the United States of America
1 2 3 4 5 6 7 04 03 02 01 00

For permission to use material from this text, contact us:
Web: http://www.thomsonrights.com
Fax: 1-800-730-2215
Phone: 1-800-730-2214

For more information, contact:
Wadsworth/Thomson Learning, Inc.
10 Davis Drive
Belmont, CA 94002-3098
USA
http://www.wadsworth.com

ISBN: 0-534-58363-6

Intrigued by the phrase, Delaney had spent an afternoon in the reading room of the 42ⁿᵈ Street library, tracking down Occam and his "Razor.". . .

"Occam was a fourteenth century philosopher," he reported. . . . "Anyway, he was famous for his hardheaded approach to problem solving. He believed in shaving away all extraneous details. . . ."

"But you've been doing that all your life, Edward."

"I guess so," he laughed, "but I call it 'Cut out the crap.'" . . .

"I wonder if old Occam ever tried solving an irrational problem by rational means. I wonder if he wouldn't begin to doubt the value of logic and deductive reasoning when you're dealing with—"

But then the door to the hospital room swung open. . .

—Lawrence Sanders, **The First Deadly Sin**

William of Ockham

Fifteenth or sixteenth century color drawing,
courtesy of the Franciscan monastery
in Cracow, Poland

Contents

1

Introduction

Most people are glad the medieval period is long behind us, and some people are aware that a philosopher named William of Ockham had a lot to do with bringing it to an end. Yet, not very many people know much about this man and his work. In recent years, Ockham's writings have become more available, and a body of excellent Ockham scholarship has developed. Nevertheless, much of the material remains accessible to only a small circle of specialists who are already familiar with the language and the concepts involved. This is a shame since Ockham is very much worth getting to know, both for understanding the history of Western thought and for understanding current themes in philosophy. In this book, we aim to introduce Ockham to the non-specialist, hoping to share our enthusiasm and encourage further study. We begin with a little bit about Ockham's life and work as a whole.

1.1 Ockham's Times

The fourteenth century was a tumultuous time in Europe. On the one hand, intellectual life was thriving. Universities, which had come into existence during the previous century, were healthy and proliferating. Among the great writers of the day were Dante Alighieri (1265-1321), Francesco de Petrarch (1304-74), and Geoffrey Chaucer (1340-1400). On the other hand, old institutions and certainties were breaking down. Such large-scale disasters as the Great Famine (1315-1322), the Hundred Years' War (1337-1453), and the plague of the Black Death (1340s-50s) contributed to the feeling that the end of the world was very close at hand. It was a time of equal opportunity for both superstition and science.

Renaissance and Enlightenment critics dubbed the spirit of the age "Gothic," meaning uncouth, uncivilized, primitive, crude. The reference was to the Goths, a barbaric Germanic tribe that contributed to the downfall of ancient Rome.

Needless to say, the term "Gothic" is just as suspect as the term "Dark Ages." True, certain important developments lay dormant during much of the Middle Ages, and the Renaissance was really a renaissance. But it is too easy to see the events that signaled the birth of modernity (the rediscovery of ancient thought, the scientific revolution, the reaction against the monolithic Church, and so on) as events suddenly arising in the fifteenth and sixteenth century out of nothing. There were significant stirrings all along, and we find in Ockham all sorts of seminal ideas. One of the enduring fascinations with Ockham, one we aim to feature in this book, is precisely the extent to which he helped lay the groundwork for a new era.

1.2 Ockham's Life

Ockham's biography makes for a truly Gothic tale, beginning with some mysteries. Nothing is known about his family. We can only assume he was an Englishman from the small town near London whose name he bears. We do not know for sure when he was born or when he died. The dates you will find in encyclopedia entries (born 1280 or 1285; died 1347 or 1349) are probably close; there is a record of his ordination in the year 1306, and his prolific writing came to an abrupt halt in the midst of the Black Death. Ockham probably spoke Middle English or French but he wrote in Latin, which is why his name is sometimes Latinized to "Occam."

Two things about Ockham of which we can be certain are that he was a Franciscan monk and that he was a graduate student at the University of Oxford. While at Oxford, he completed nearly all the requirements for a doctorate and transformed the way philosophy was done there for generations to come. Yet he never received his degree. In 1323, he was summoned to the papal court at Avignon. Four years later, we find him facing fifty-six charges of heresy. His accusers were unable to make their case stick.

But Ockham's brush with the criminal element changed the course of his life. After meeting some other Franciscans awaiting trial in Avignon, Ockham undertook an investigation into Pope John XXII's recent pronouncements on poverty in monastic orders. He describes his reaction in a letter:

In these so-called pronouncements I found a great many things that are heretical, erroneous, stupid, ridiculous, fantastic, insane and defamatory. They are patently perverse and equally contrary to orthodox faith, good morals, natural reason, certain experience, and brotherly love. [OPol III 6; K 3-4. *For an explanation of this and other bibliographical notes, consult the Bibliography at the back of this book.*]

There was no going back. On May 26, 1328, when it had become clear that Ockham and his friends were in grave danger, they escaped into the night, to the court of Emperor Louis of Bavaria, who was himself a powerful opponent of the Pope. They were all excommunicated. After a brief and unsuccessful campaign in Italy, the Emperor and his entourage retired to Munich. Ockham spent the rest of his days there as a kind of political activist.

A bit about the chronology and content of his works may be helpful. In the Middle Ages, there were three choices for graduate school: medicine, law, or theology. Philosophers, including Ockham, were trained in the last. Until well into the Renaissance, standard curriculum in faculties of theology all across Europe involved lecturing on a four-volume text called *The Sentences* by Peter Lombard. It presented arguments for and against various opinions, thereby providing an ideal forum for philosophical discussion. Ockham's lectures on all four books have been preserved and they are among his earliest works, dating from around 1317-9. Another standard academic procedure Ockham took part in before the Avignon affair was public debate on disputed questions. Notes on these, along with his commentaries on various works of Aristotle and other special treatises, were probably written during and just after his lectureship, in the early 1320s. As his work became increasingly controversial, Ockham participated in a special kind of debate known as the "Quodlibetal" (meaning "whatever you like"), in which the disputant was asked to answer questions of interest to the audience. These may have been recorded just prior to or during the Avignon affair, in the mid-1320s. Then we have Ockham's massive *Summa Logicae.* It is probably the latest of his non-political works, and may have been composed in part after the exodus to Munich. The political works, which began to appear in the late 1320s, are all very polemical. They include such items as a pamphlet enumerating the errors of the Pope, the *Short Discourse on Tyrannical Government,* which mysteriously cuts off mid-sentence, and the more than six-hundred page *Dialogue* concerning the power of the pope and the emperor.

1.3 The Aristotle Factor

There is a good deal in this book about Aristotle (384-322 B.C.). One needs to understand what Aristotle was to the medievals in order to understand Ockham.

During the early Middle Ages, only two of Aristotle's works were available in Latin, both treatises on logic. Increasing interest in logic during the twelfth century led to the rediscovery of more of Aristotle's logic. Soon, logic was no longer enough. By the thirteenth century, several Aristotelian treatises on a broad range of subjects were circulating, many being adopted as required reading in the newly founded universities. Aristotle became known as "The Philosopher."

Whereas Aristotle's logic was more or less religiously neutral, much of his other work was not. Unsurprisingly, Aristotle, who pre-dated Jesus by a few hundred years, occasionally does not appear to mesh terribly well with Christian doctrine. For example, Aristotle's God, the "Unmoved Mover," was more like a force of nature than a creator or a savior. Church leaders, who had considerable control over what went on in the schools, were concerned. They had two options: ban Aristotle as anathema, or encourage people to read Aristotle in ways that made him consistent with the faith. They chose the latter.

By and large, late medieval Aristotle enthusiasts accepted—even rather enjoyed—this challenge. Thomas Aquinas (1225-1274) is a famous example. He used Aristotle's ideas to develop theological doctrines that became orthodoxy ever after.

Ockham's case is different. He used Aristotle to develop philosophical doctrines that were often at odds both with mainstream interpretations of Aristotle and with positions of the Church. Sometimes, Ockham seems to use The Philosopher as an excuse to consider ideas that would otherwise not have been acceptable to explore.

Take, for example, Ockham's commentary on Aristotle's *Physics*. It begins with the curious disclaimer that readers should attribute anything that may sound heretical in this work to Aristotle rather than to Ockham. He writes,

> For I do not intend to present what I myself approve in accordance with the Catholic faith, but only what I think The Philosopher held—or at least ought to have held, as it seems to me, according to his own principles. [OPh IV, 3-4; B 2-3]

Ockham goes on to say that Aristotle, who did not have to reconcile his views with the Catholic faith, held these positions more firmly and consistently than Ockham himself could.

4

So the relation of Ockham to Aristotle turns out to be a complicated one. Ockham is doing three (sometimes rather incompatible) things at once with The Philosopher: trying to understanding the difficult things Aristotle really meant to say; interpreting Aristotle in a way consistent with fourteenth-century Christian doctrine; and finding his own positions in Aristotle's writings.

The main point to keep in mind is that, for better or for worse, Ockham considered himself an Aristotelian. Our goal in this book is not to assess the validity of this claim, but rather, to appreciate the unique brand of Aristotelianism Ockham has to offer.

1.4 The Razor: Popular Version

If you heard anything at all about Ockham prior to opening this book, chances are you heard about *Ockham's Razor*, the famous principle of parsimony or simplicity so often appealed to in philosophy, science, and the occasional Hollywood movie (most recently in *Contact* [1997] and *Good Will Hunting* [1998]).

The principle of parsimony provides one criterion for choice among competing theories or explanations. It says that when competing theories are equally adequate according to the other criteria, one should choose the simplest theory.

This principle was not called a "razor" by Ockham; the name is of a much more modern origin. And calling the principle "Ockham's" might mislead, since it was used as a criterion for theorizing long before him, and has been used since his time in ways that he would hardly authorize. Nevertheless, the principle is appropriately called "Ockham's Razor," because the metaphor of cutting or trimming captures something essential to Ockham's approach.

At its most basic level, parsimonious theorizing is just common sense. Suppose that, one morning, when you go out to fetch the newspaper from your doorstep, it is not there. You can imagine any number of explanations to account for this. Maybe the delivery person overslept. Maybe that particular newspaper was made out of a soluble material and dissolved in the rain. Maybe aliens stole it. Reasonable people would pick the first. It is "simpler" because the others require postulation of additional entities in our universe: soluble newspapers, aliens.

This reasoning looks like a use of Ockham's Razor as it is often expressed by the slogan, *"Entia non sunt multiplicanda praeter necesitatem"* ("Beings should not be multiplied beyond necessity"). But Ockham's Razor should not be thought of primarily as a tool for minimizing entities.

For one thing, always opting for the least number of entities is not likely to be conducive toward truth. After all, *solipsism*, the view that the self is the only thing that exists, postulates the least possible number of things. It is maximally simple, and clearly false. The world has clearly shown itself to be a complex multitude of many different kinds of things, altogether "lush, prodigal, messy, wasteful, sexy, etc.," (as D. L. Gunner famously put it).

Further, reducing the number of entities we believe in often comes with the cost of increasing the complexity of the principles on which those entities behave. A solipsist believes in only one thing, but it is *very* complicated!

To the extent that Ockham's Razor has been interpreted as a "principle of stinginess," it has been rightly rejected. But Ockham never said *"Entia non sunt multiplicanda praeter necesitatem,"* nor does this aptly describe the simplifying methodology he so often employs.

1.5 The Razor: Ockham's Version

What is operating in the rational, conservative, explanation of choice in the newspaper example is not precisely minimization of entities. What we do, rather, is consider everything we know already about how things happen and are likely to happen, and see whether all this is sufficient to account for the matter at hand. If it is, then it would be sloppy thinking to add yet another explanation on top. According to this approach, we do not attribute simplicity to the world but merely aim for simplicity in our understanding of the world. This is the advice we find in the two main versions of the Razor actually found in Ockham's writing: *"Pluralitas non est ponenda sine necessitate"* ("Plurality should not be posited without necessity") [e.g., OTh IV 322]; and *"Frustra fit per plura quod potest fieri per pauciora"* ("It is useless to do with more what can be done with less") [e.g., OTh X 157].

That Ockham means to check the unruly proliferation of explanation becomes clearer in the second formulation, where talk of "positing less" is replaced by "doing with less." The idea is that we *do* things with theories, namely, describe and predict, and we can do this better if we avoid complexity wherever possible. Ockham is careful to make sure that his philosophical theories account for all of the obvious phenomena of everyday life; but the object is always to make do, in these theories, with as few assumptions and explanatory devices as possible.

The principle of parsimony is what enabled Ockham to scrape away the encrusted ideologies of the Middle Ages. It was a small tool that made a very big difference, as we shall see in the pages to follow.

2
Nominalism

Ockham's central philosophical technique is his application of the Razor: using the criterion of simplicity as a test for the adequacy of theories. The technique of seeking simplification can be applied in any area of philosophy, but Ockham's best known application of the Razor is in metaphysics, on the problem of universals. One solution to this problem is *nominalism*, and this is the position that Ockham became famous for defending. In this chapter, we will see how Ockham's nominalism develops out of his maverick interpretation of Aristotle.

2.1 Substances

The most basic question in metaphysics is, "What is there?" The obvious answer is that there are all sorts of particular things: this strawberry, the neighbor's cat, the moon, and so on. Philosophers sometimes call such objects "substances."

Each substance has a variety of different characteristics: *qualities*, and *relations* to other things. Tabitha's qualities include that she is gray and furry, and her relations include that she is on the mat and that she is smaller than you.

In his *Physics*, Aristotle elaborated this common sense idea into a philosophical theory. Every substance, according to his theory, is a compound of form (characteristics) plus matter (what these characteristics are characteristics of). This way of thinking about substances has come to be known as *hylomorphism.*

Ockham was a hylomorphist. He accepted Aristotle's matter/form distinction, along with the thesis that matter is the more basic of the two. Relations depend on matter because it is the individual parcels of matter that are related; qualities depend on matter because they *inhere* in the matter.

Hylomorphism is very useful for describing things in the world and how they change. Nevertheless, it led to a problem.

2.2 The Problem of Universals

Consider Hypatia and Heraclitus, two humans, and Rover, their dog. Hylomorphism tells us that they are three substances, each consisting in an individual parcel of matter, each with its own individual form.

Hylomorphism does not, however, explain why two of the substances are "the same" and the other is "different." Hypatia and Heraclitus are both human, and Rover is not. Hypatia and Heraclitus are the same *kind* of thing.

Do *kinds of things* exist in addition to things? We of course have ideas of kinds in our minds, but do kinds exist outside the mind in the external world? If so, then what exactly are they? If not, then how do we come to make judgements about sameness? The problem of explaining how it is that individual things are of the same kind is the *problem of universals*.

2.3 Realism About Universals

There are a variety of possible solutions. We might want to say that Hypatia and Heraclitus share something that Rover does not. We know what sharing is like. When Howard and Hilda share an apartment, there is a third thing—the apartment—that both of them are related to in certain ways, in this case, by living in it, using its facilities, and so on. Should we imagine that Hypatia and Heraclitus share some third thing in this sense? What is this third thing? It must be *humanness*.

This way of understanding universals comes from Plato (427-347 B.C.) and is called *transcendent realism*. According to this view, the forms of *humanness, doghood, rockhood, greenness*, and so on, are universals that exist beyond ("transcend") the particular individuals in the world. Although Hypatia and Heraclitus share in *humanness*, *humanness* is an abstract thing that exists independently of them. *Humanness* would exist even if no humans existed. Positing the existence of transcendent universal forms explains how it is that individuals are of the same kind.

By Ockham's day, however, transcendent realism had fallen into disrepute. It seems to generate more problems then it solves. Plato's abstract forms are peculiar entities. Whereas human beings have locations, *humanness* does not. Platonists sometimes say that these forms exist "in another realm," perhaps in a supernatural realm, but, in that case, it is not at all clear how we know about them. We can see particular human beings, but never *humanness*. Another problem concerns the relation between forms and particulars. We can specify the relation between Howard and Hilda and their apartment, but how are Hypatia and Heraclitus related to *humanness*? Saying, with the Platonists, that humans "participate" in *humanness* is not much help.

Most late medievals thought that Aristotle had definitively refuted transcendent realism. They took him to have proposed an alternative view, according to which universal forms such as *humanness* exist, not in some other realm, but rather, wholly within particular human beings. This view, like Plato's, is *realism* about universals, because it asserts that universals exist outside the mind, but it is nowadays called *moderate realism*, because it is supposed not to be as metaphysically profligate as transcendent realism. Another name for this view is *immanent realism*, because it holds that universals are immanent within material objects.

Moderate realists do not hold merely that things are sortable into kinds; nobody would deny this. They hold that the world contains more than just the particular individuals we see. It contains universal entities that are shared among individuals. Although *humanness* would not exist if no humans existed, *humanness* does exist in and among humans.

Is moderate realism the best way to solve the problem of universals? It is not clear that Aristotle ever settled this question in his own mind. Thomas Aquinas adopted this view, and saw Aristotle as endorsing it. Most Aristotle interpreters ever since have accepted moderate realism as the correct interpretation of The Philosopher. Ockham, however, saw moderate realism as an enormous mistake, and preferred to think that Aristotle rejected it.

Ockham maintains that forms are absolutely particular characteristics, and that there is no such reality as universals outside the mind. This idea, that the world consists entirely of individual substances, each with its own unique matter and form, is what Ockham was looking for in Aristotle. He resists the realist turn by simply denying that Hypatia and Heraclitus must have something literally in common in order to be called "human."

2.4 Ockham Against Realism

Ockham's complaint against realism about universals, found throughout his works, is that it is blatantly incoherent. He writes,

> There is no universal outside the mind really existing in individual substances or in the essences of things. . . . The reason is that everything that is not many things is necessarily one thing in number and consequently a singular thing. [OPh II 11-2]

The universal *humanness* is supposed to be one thing, and yet, if it is one thing, how can it be common to many?

Moderate realists claim that a single universal inheres in many separate individuals. This cannot be true, Ockham reasons, because anything that is wholly in one thing cannot be wholly in another. A log, for example, can be immersed both in air and in water, but cannot be immersed wholly in both at the same time.

We might be tempted to explain what it is for two things to be human by saying that they both belong to the same big collection—the set of all humans, including all times and all places. We thus distinguish the collection of humans from the particular things that belong in this collection. But this leaves us with the original question: why do Hypatia and Heraclitus belong to this collection while Rover does not?

When moderate realists talk about *humanness*, they are not talking about the collection of all humans, separated in time and space. *Humanness* is wholly in Hypatia and wholly in Heraclitus. What makes it the case that a particular thing belongs to the collection of humans? The realists' answer is that each individual in this collection shares in a universal entity, *humanness*, and nothing outside this collection shares in that entity. This entity must inhere wholly in each object, because each object is fully human.

Some critics of realism ground their argument against immanent universal forms in the claim that it is impossible for a single thing to be two different places at once. They ask, how can *humanness* be in Hypatia over here while at the same time being in Heraclitus way over there? But realists rightly object to this strategy as ad hoc. They simply reply that they define universals in the first place as things that can be in many different places at once.

But Ockham concedes to moderate realists that it is possible for a single thing to be in many different places at once. As a matter of fact, he finds an instance of this phenomenon in transubstantiation, the changing of bread and wine into the body and blood of Christ. Every time a Catholic priest performs the sacrament of communion anywhere in the world, Jesus himself, whole and entire, becomes present there. [See e.g., OTh IX 360-1; Q 299 and OTh IX 422; Q 348.]

Ockham denies, however, that it is possible for a single thing to *inhere* in two separate things at the same time. To be in a place can be understood minimally as exerting an effect there. In this sense, calling someone on the telephone is a way of being present there. But to inhere in something is more than merely exerting an effect at a location. To inhere is to become identical with the thing at that location. If something called "humanness" inheres in Hypatia, then that thing *is* Hypatia. So if Hypatia is sad at the moment, then *humanness* is sad. But *humanness* also inheres in Heraclitus, and Heraclitus is not sad. So humanness is sad and not sad at the same time, which really is a contradiction.

Ockham insists that each particular object has its own particular characteristics, different from the characteristics of others. This goes for "essential" characteristics, like being human, as well as "accidental" characteristics, like hair color. Hypatia's hair color is wholly in Hypatia; it is not in anyone else. Heraclitus's hair color is a numerically distinct characteristic. By this, Ockham does not necessarily mean that one can distinguish a difference between the two colors. Even if Hypatia's hair color is utterly indistinguishable from Heraclitus's, they are not literally the one and the same thing. We are talking about two separate items: Hypatia's hair color is here, and Heraclitus's hair color is there.

2.5 Hypostatization

Ockham attacks every version of metaphysical realism he can lay his hands on. At bottom, in his view, all of them commit an unnecessary and problematic *hypostatization*. To hypostatize is to attribute real and independent existence to something. Ockham's message is that philosophers should not hypostatize universals.

The method of hypostatizing things in order to solve philosophical problems runs directly contrary to the principle of parsimony, and Ockham finds many occasions for criticizing it throughout his work. His favorite criticism involves an appeal to what we will call the *Divine Annihilation Principle*:

> If *x* is a real thing existing independently of *y*, then God should be able to destroy *x* without destroying *y*.

Ockham points out that, according to realism,

> it would follow that God would not be able to annihilate one individual substance without destroying the other individuals

11

of the same kind. For, if he were to annihilate one individual, he would destroy the whole that is essentially that individual and, consequently, he would destroy the universal that is in it and in others of the same essence. Other things of the same essence would not remain, for they could not continue to exist without the universal that constitutes a part of them. [OPh I 51]

His argument is this. If *humanness* inheres in Hypatia, then it is identical to Hypatia. So, when Hypatia is destroyed, *humanness* should be destroyed. It is not destroyed, however, because Heraclitus survives, and he is identical to *humanness* too.

In response to this difficulty, some realists claimed that individuals are related to universals in a way that constitutes neither strict identity nor absolute difference. John Duns Scotus (1265-1308), who was one of the most sophisticated medieval defenders of immanent realism, says that one's particular nature and one's common nature are "formally distinct." [J 484] In making this distinction, Scotus identifies: (1) Hypatia's individual self (famously called by him "*haecceitas*" meaning "thisness"), which is destroyed when she is because it is shared by nobody else; and (2) Hypatia's universal self, which survives her death because it is shared by all other humans. This universal self or common nature is *humanness*. It is neither strictly identical to her (as her individual self is) nor absolutely different from her (as her apartment is).

So Scotus has not only hypostatized an *x* but has hypostatized a very peculiar sort of *x*. How can *x* be related to *y* in such a way that *x* is neither the same as *y* nor different from *y*? Granted, Scotus would say, nothing in the visible world has this peculiarity about it, but a form is a principle of nature, and we can expect such things to be unlike anything we experience.

It is at this point in the argument that Ockham wields his razor. He agrees that if we cannot avoid positing peculiar principles then we must posit peculiar principles. But is there a way to avoid it? Ockham was sure that there is. His alternative is known as "nominalism," from the Latin word "*nomen*" meaning "name," because it holds that members of a kind do not share anything between them other than a written or spoken name and its corresponding concept in the mind.

2.6 Subjectivism

Ockham's nominalism is anti-realist in that it denies that kinds exist outside the mind, but it is not *subjectivist*. Subjectivists about kinds hold that our classifications are arbitrary individual or social constructs.

Ockham knew of subjectivism through the anti-realist Roscelin (born c. 1045). In the midst of a discussion of the nature of universals, Ockham writes,

> There could be an opinion according to which nothing is universal by nature but only by convention, in the same way that a word is universal by convention. [OTh I 271]

This version of subjectivism is called *conventionalism*. Ockham dismisses it as untenable, and does not bother with arguments since it was not at all popular among his contemporaries.

Conventionalism does seem implausible, at least when it comes to sorting natural objects. A good deal of science consists in discovering the right categories in which to classify things. If it were merely a matter of conventional division, then science would never be disproven. We (as a society) could just decide arbitrarily upon any old categories, and they would be as good as any others. But in reality, science revises its categories to account for the facts.

A more plausible version of subjectivism that is popular today is *innatism*. It holds that categories are born within us, a feature of the hard wiring of our brains. This makes the classifications we impose more universal, and more inevitable, and might serve to explain the fact that vastly different societies, despite great differences in social convention, categorize many things in much the same way. In the process of evolution, those who could distinguish rocks from mangos would have reproduced a lot more successfully than those who could not. Hence, over eons, this trait has become dominant in the human species.

Innatism is subjectivist in so far as it holds that categorization results from the way our minds work, rather than from the way the external world is. If we happened to have evolved with a different set of innate mental categories, then that would be the "right" way to see the world. In a way, this view also makes categorization arbitrary, and Ockham would reject it.

If categories are not arbitrary, and if they do not correspond to external kinds, then what is their objective basis?

2.7 Similarity

According to Ockham, the fact that Hypatia and Heraclitus are both human is not merely a matter of how we see them. He takes the common-sense view for granted. There really is something about Hypatia and Heraclitus, independent of how we see them, that accounts for their both being human. They are objectively similar. Ockham writes,

The intellect no more makes it the case that white Socrates is similar to Plato than it makes it the case that Socrates is white. Indeed, Socrates is similar to Plato by the very fact that Socrates is white and Plato is white apart from any conceptualization. And so the intellect does nothing to make it the case that Socrates is similar to Plato. Yet, despite this, the intellect can capture these absolutely distinct things under a single concept. It can express an absolute concept, as when one says simply "Socrates is white," or "Plato is white." Or it can express a relative concept, as when one says "Socrates is similar to Plato with respect to *whiteness*." And this relative concept *whiteness* exists only in the mind. [OTh IX 679; Q 572]

We do not need to posit any universals in things in order to make color judgements objective. Things cause universal judgments in the mind when they are similar.

Recall that, according to hylomorphism, there are two kinds of characteristics: relations and qualities. Ockham had a nominalist way of understanding each of these. Relations, such as *on the mat*, are judgements in the mind, much like universals. [See OTh IX 611-18; Q 512-18.] So, *on the mat* does not inhere in Tabitha. Qualities, on the other hand, do inhere in substances. This is because qualities are causal powers of things. Grey is the way Tabitha is reflecting light or the way that she would reflect light were light shining on her. Thinking of qualities as causal powers helps to explain Ockham's objectivism.

Heraclitus has characteristics with the power to cause the concept of *humanness* to enter the mind of those he meets. When people are in the presence of Heraclitus, he causes them to think a certain thought. When people are in the presence of Hypatia she causes them to think an exactly similar thought. When people are in the presence of Rover, he does not cause them to think this thought.

Of course, the human mind is very complex. You might think of *humanness* while in the presence of Rover. In Ockham's view, however, Rover would not have caused this. Rather, this would be a case of Rover triggering a memory of the concept caused by individuals like Hypatia and Heraclitus. Likewise, Hypatia and Heraclitus might cause you to think a large number of thoughts, and you may not even be consciously aware of your thought of *humanness* every time you are in their presence. When you are making judgements about natural kinds, however, this is precisely the sort of thought you turn to.

Do we need to posit a single thing within both Heraclitus and Hypatia in order to explain why they cause the people they meet to think of *humanness*? Not at all. Suppose that Hypatia has an ulcer and that there are two things that irritate it, sauerkraut and Heraclitus. Sauerkraut and Heraclitus are not the same at all. Nevertheless they both cause ulcer irritation. They have similar causal powers, because they both cause similar things. We can imagine them causing different but exactly similar irritations, as when Hypatia eats sauerkraut on Tuesday, has a stomach ache that goes away, and then on Wednesday talks to Heraclitus only to get another stomach ache. Likewise, Plato and Socrates are not the same at all, even though they both cause certain thoughts—of *humanness*, of *whiteness*, etc. Suppose Socrates caused a white-thought in you on Tuesday, and Plato caused a white-thought in you on Wednesday. This is why you say that Socrates and Plato are both white. According to Ockham, the members of a kind share nothing between them, but they do have very similar effects on the mind.

Ockham's nominalism stands at the very center of his thought. He did not invent it: varieties of this view can be found in several philosophers of his age, and earlier. He himself claims to have found it in Aristotle. Nevertheless, he is arguably the strongest, clearest, most systematic, and most influential proponent of this position who ever lived. After he died, Ockham became known as "The Venerable Inceptor." An "inceptor" was a student who had completed almost all of the requirements for becoming a master of theology. The term applies to Ockham because that is as far as he got before his career was interrupted. His nominalist followers, however, came to take this designation also in the sense of "initiator," referring to Ockham as the source of the nominalist movement. Western philosophy, especially in the Anglo-American tradition, shows strong currents of nominalism ever since, and Ockham's influence is pivotal in this.

3
The Stages of Knowledge

Every philosopher who constructs a metaphysical theory, a general account of what there is, does so with an eye to epistemology, a general account of how *we know* what there is. According to Ockham's nominalist metaphysics, the world contains only singular, particular individuals. It seems obvious that we know that these things exist and what they are like because we perceive them. For Ockham, this is the starting-point. He explains the process of coming to know things about the world as a series of steps. In this chapter, we will trace these steps, showing how Ockham accounts for various different kinds of knowledge and error.

3.1 The Origin of Ideas of Particular Things

According to Ockham's epistemology, the first step of knowledge acquisition is *sensory cognition*. It can be understood as the passive reception of an internal effect from an outside cause. The mind does not yet conceptualize—i.e., categorize—its objects, or make any judgment about them at all. In fact, it is a bit misleading to call sensory cognition "cognition" because nothing is believed or known yet. Think of it as what a camera is capable of.

Sensory cognition is a power human beings have in common with animals. Although an earthworm reacts to sunlight (by heading back into the dark) it presumably does not formulate the thought, "There's the sun; better get out of here!" It merely registers and reacts to the data.

The second step of knowledge acquisition is called *intuitive cognition*. An intuitive cognition is the first real thought one has about an object of perception. What is this thought like? Suppose you see something. After registering visual data, you immediately make a judgement, as Ockham says,

> whether the thing exists or not in such a way that if the thing exists, the intellect immediately judges it to exist and evidently knows that it exists, unless by chance it is impeded due to some flaw in the cognitive act. [OTh I 31]

You are thinking that there is something out there. Suppose you decide to call it "Wangdoodle." Then, in virtue of intuitive cognition, you are making the judgement, "Wangdoodle exists."

You are perceiving Wangdoodle, including all its particular characteristics, so you are also, at the same time, thinking about *how* Wangdoodle exists. It has a certain color, for example. Once you give a name to this color, say "glurph," you are making the judgement, not just that Wangdoodle is, but that it is glurph. You may also make the judgement that Wangdoodle is a certain distance from you. In Ockham's words,

> Intuitive cognition is such that when some things are cognized, of which one inheres in the other, or one is spatially distant from the other, or exists in some relation to the other, immediately in virtue of that non-propositional cognition of those things, it is known if the thing inheres or does not inhere, if it is spatially distant or not, and the same for other true contingent propositions, unless that cognition is flawed or there is some impediment. [OTh I 31]

No general concepts or categorizations are involved in intuitive cognition; all judgements concern particular things and their particular characteristics. The concepts you are applying here are *individual* concepts: they apply only to this individual thing.

3.2 The Origin of General Ideas

An intuitive cognition is just as much an *apprehension* (i.e., a direct awareness or perception) of the external object as a sensory cognition is. So, under ordinary circumstances, you will have intuitive cognitions only of things that really exist before you. Nevertheless, it is possible to have beliefs about Wangdoodle while not in its presence. How does this work?

One way is that you remember it. Ockham calls this *recordative cognition*. A recordative cognition of Wangdoodle, like an intuitive cognition of it, is caused by Wangdoodle. The difference is that the recordative cognition is more distant along the causal chain; it is the result of an earlier intuitive cognition.

There is more to cognition than this, however. In addition to individual concepts that apply singly to individuals, you have general concepts that apply to things *as members of a group.* The thought "Wangdoodle is glurph" is much less likely than "There's a brown cow." Clearly, nominalists have to account for our ability to use general concepts like *brown* and *cow.* They cannot rely, as realists can, on our apprehension of external universals to account for the origin of abstract concepts. Where, then, do we get them?

According to Ockham, these concepts are generated in the mind through *abstractive cognition.* He writes that "abstractive cognition presupposes an intuitive cognition with respect to the same object, and . . . is not proper to the singular; it is not just sometimes, but always, a shared cognition." [OTh IX 74; Q 65] When you perceive more than one singular, and recognize a similarity between the resulting intuitive cognitions, you form a concept that applies, and hence "belongs," equally to both.

Imagine you have had intuitive cognitions of various objects other than just Wangdoodle. You notice some similarities and differences among them. Wangdoodle resembles some of the things in color, but not others. So, you decide to use the name "glurph" to apply to all the things that are similar to Wangdoodle colorwise. Now the word "glurph" that you used before as the name of Wangdoodle's individual color, has come to be used to apply a general concept. It is a concept that is shared by a number of things. When you run into something new, you can call it "glurph" (or "not-glurph") too, applying (or denying) the general concept to it. In much the same way, remembered particular experiences of Wangdoodle can be generalized for other individuals judged sufficiently similar.

3.3 Ockham and Empiricism

Ockham's explanation of knowledge acquisition strongly resembles that of the famous Enlightenment philosophers John Locke (1632-1704), George Berkeley (1685-1753), and David Hume (1711-1776). He, like them, and long before them, was an *empiricist*: he locates the origin of individual and general ideas in perceptual experience; he denies that concepts are innate; he boldly asserts that human beings enter the world as "blank slates" (*tabula rasa*). [OPh IV 23-4]

But Ockham's empiricism is presented in a medieval way. At one point, he appears to deny the claim that all ideas arise from sense experience. Angels, he claims, have no bodies of their own, so they are incapable of sensation; yet, they are able to know things about the external world. [See Quod 4.9.] Where did they get the concepts necessary for knowledge?

Most medievals talked with straight faces about angels. Aquinas, in fact, speculated endlessly about their natures. It would be a mistake, however, to dismiss all of this as primitive superstition. Ockham uses angels as a thought-experiment. Just as contemporary philosophers sometimes consider Martians, or dwellers on a parallel twin-earth in order to imagine what is possible, Ockham considers angels.

What Ockham thinks follows from the angel thought-experiment is that intuitive cognition is possible without sensory cognition. There is nothing in the idea of an intuitive cognition that implies that an intuitive cognition *has to* arise from the data provided by sensory cognition.

Ockham establishes this point by appealing to a principle that appears regularly in his arguments: For any x and y where x causes y, God can cause y directly without the help of x. Ockham uses this principle to show that the empiricist account of knowledge acquisition is a contingent fact about human beings. He writes,

> Every effect that God is able to produce by the mediation of a secondary cause he is able to produce by himself without mediation. God is able to produce an intuitive cognition of a physical thing by the mediation of a physical object. Therefore, he is able to produce this cognition without mediation, by himself. [OTh IX 605; Q 506]

For Ockham, God's omnipotence is limited to the logically possible. So he uses the distinction between what God can and cannot do as a way of talking about what is logically possible and what is not. Here, he is claiming that God could supply an intuitive cognition directly to a human mind without the help of the external physical objects through which we normally receive intuitive cognitions; it is not necessary that cognitions arise from perception of externals.

This claim might appear decidedly anti-empiricist, but in fact it is not. The British Empiricists claim that all our ideas in fact arise from sensation, but they need not claim that it is unimaginable or in some sense impossible for them to arise without sensation. It is possible that there might be another kind of mind that got its ideas in some other way. And Hume would, of course, be entirely sympathetic to Ockham's view that the causal connection is not a necessary one.

3.4 Realism and Representationalism

Many philosophers today are *representationalist* empiricists. According to representationalism, our perceptual contact with the outside world causes internal *sense-impressions*, mental entities that represent external objects, and that provide evidence for the way the world is.

Peter Aureol (1275-1322) was a pioneering representationalist. While addressing an abstruse question about the Trinity, Aureol asserts that the Word of God is a representational emanation from the Son of God that is so objective that it "truly and really seizes being of its own." He goes on to claim that in every instance of understanding, the thing being understood emanates a representation in virtue of which it becomes an object in the intellect. [Aureol's position, here and in the following, are reported by Ockham, OTh IV 230-8.]

Aureol's philosophical motivation for this view comes from the problem of sensory deception. He offers many examples, including one familiar from subsequent literature. When you immerse a straight stick half into water, it appears bent at the point of immersion. The stick is not bent; everyone knows that sticks do not bend when you immerse them in water. What, then, is bent? Aureol asks. Not the stick out there. It must be the visual impression you have inside you. Aureol calls this an "apparition" and modern philosophers have called it a "sense datum."

Representationalists hold that in all visual perception, it is the representation that is directly, immediately apprehended. The representation stands as an intermediary between the external object and your judgement about it. So the judgement about what is out there is inferred from the representation, which is evidence for it.

Notoriously, representationalism leads to difficult or insoluble skeptical difficulties. We must have reasons to think that x counts as evidence, in order to justify the belief in y on the basis of x. What reason do we have, however, to think that sense-impressions ever show anything at all about the external world? Since sense-impressions sometimes give misleading evidence about the external world, doubts can be raised about the conclusion drawn from any of them.

The obvious way to show that something really is evidence is to demonstrate a correlation between the evidence and the thing for which it provides evidence. In order to show, for example, that dark clouds provide some evidence that it is going to rain, one has to show that they tend to be followed by rain. So, in the case of representationalism, we would have to show that our sense-impressions often are connected with the external objects for which they supposedly provide evidence.

This, however, is impossible. If all our information about the external world comes from perception, and if all perception is mediated by these internal sense-impressions, then we will *never* be able to discover a correlation between a sense-impression and the external world. The only thing we could do to verify whether any sense-impression gave reliable information would be to check another sense-impression. But then we would have to verify it as well, and so on, and so on.

The representationalist picture of perception, then, leads to the notorious problem of the existence of the external world. This is the problem that sometimes makes non-philosophers feel some puzzlement (if not actual disdain) about philosophy. Any philosopher who comes to the conclusion that there is no external world must be short a couple of marbles. There is a serious question here, however. Where did the representationalist's reasoning go wrong? How are we to understand the process by which we acquire knowledge so as to justify our confidence in our beliefs about the external world?

Ockham thinks the representationalists go wrong in positing mental entities. He denies that perception is mediated by sense-impressions. Rejecting representationalism entirely, Ockham adopts, instead, a version of *direct realism*.

Note that the term "realism" has a different meaning in this context. Ockham opposes *metaphysical* realism, the view that universals exist outside the mind. In the present context, however, we are referring instead to *epistemological* realism. This is the position that we perceive the world directly, without a mediating representation. According to this view, the entities that are the immediate objects in perception are the ordinary cows and people and so on that exist in the world. Representationalism, in contrast, is anti-realist: its objects of perception are mind-dependent subjective entities.

Representationalists consider sensory cognition as the process in which an external object produces an "apparition" inside us. Ockham would insist that this is misleading. Why suppose that some *thing* is produced? What happens is this: the mind is being affected in a certain way (sensory cognition), and we come to believe that there is something out there causing this effect (intuitive cognition). There is no subjective entity mediating between mind and world.

Direct realism enables Ockham to account for the bent-stick illusion without representations. When you see a straight stick half-immersed in water, a straight stick is affecting your mind. This does not, however, guarantee that you come to believe, through intuitive cognition, that there is a straight stick out there. The water is affecting your mind too. The object of the belief is the straight stick in water. As it happens, seeing a straight stick in water has an effect on the mind that is similar to the effect caused by a bent stick. The mind always relies on similarity to make judgements. This is how we arrive at the bent-stick category in the first place. In this case, however, the similarity only goes so far. When you look closely or pull the stick out of the water you see the dissimilarity. Hence, you conclude that the concept *bent* does not apply. What, then, is bent? Nothing. Ockham writes,

> It can be conceded that "through an apparition something appears," and that "there is an apparition in the intellect," and that "something appears in the intellect." It does not follow from this language, however, that some *thing* comes to exist in the understanding. In creation, something is created. Nevertheless, *the creating* does not itself turn into such a being. It is in the same way that in the intellect "something is understood," and "something appears." [OTh IV 252]

We might come to believe that there is a bent stick there, and so, in a sense, a bent stick "appears in the intellect." Nevertheless, it is unnecessary, and therefore undesirable, to *hypostatize* sense-impressions—to count them as things.

It seems that Aureol's theory offers no advantage over Ockham's in explaining sensory deception. Ockham felt justified, therefore, in maintaining the more economical theory.

3.5 Perceptual Error and Skepticism

The problem for the representationalist was to justify the belief that our representations usually represent the world accurately. Ockham avoids this problem, but runs into another: how to justify our belief that intuitive cognition usually provides knowledge.

Some philosophers hold that beliefs may be "evident" in the sense that they guarantee their own truth: there is something about the belief itself that shows that it is infallible. If this were the case, then, all we would need to do to find out that a belief is true is to notice that it has this characteristic. When René Descartes (1596-1650) refers to "clear and distinct" ideas, he has something like this in mind.

Ockham, on the other hand, denies that positing the quality "evident" provides a solution to the problem. For him, if a belief is true and caused in the right way, then it is "evident," in the sense that it counts as knowledge. We surely have a large number of beliefs of this sort. There is nothing we can notice about these beliefs, however, to distinguish them infallibly from the false ones. Examples such as those

Aureol presents make it clear that, sometimes, intuitive cognition does arrive at false judgements. So, we might ask Ockham: why should we ever think that they are true? Maybe there is no external world out there at all. Maybe God or some powerful demon is deceiving us about the whole thing. We can raise skeptical doubts against Ockham's direct realism parallel to those we raised against the representationalist.

Ockham readily concedes that it is possible for God to fool us by producing false experiences of an external world. To deny this would be to deny God's omnipotence. [See Quod 6.6.] This is Ockham's way of saying that the existence and nature of the external world does not logically follow from the nature of our experience.

Primarily because Ockham refuses to countenance a notion of evident cognition that would preclude even God from deceiving us, his epistemology was once widely regarded as excessively skeptical. It is now generally agreed, however, that there is little in Ockham's work that promotes skepticism. He never urged us to question our belief in the external world. Neither was he interested in finding something deeper and more certain upon which to ground our beliefs. Unlike some other philosophers, Ockham did not take his job to be to prove the obvious. He took his philosophical task, rather, as something different: to organize these beliefs into a single, simple, all-encompassing theory.

There is a certain irony here. Many people think of medieval philosophers as arguing endlessly about useless questions such as the number of angels capable of dancing on the head of a pin. As we have seen, however, Ockham's avoidance of skepticism and his concentration on questions that might be answerable represents just the opposite tendency.

4

Science

Ockham maintains that human cognition is concerned with singular individuals. Nevertheless, he also recognizes that knowledge *properly speaking* requires systemization. Echoing Aristotle, he writes,

> From sense comes memory, from memory, experience, and through experience we arrive at the universal, which is the principle of the arts and sciences. [OPh IV 45]

A nominalist epistemology is not complete until it includes an account of science.

Aristotelian realists have an explanation of science ready to hand. For them, universals exist as the essences within things. Since the universal *pumpkinhood* inheres in each and every individual pumpkin, our knowledge of pumpkins-in-general can be said to come from the encounter with individual pumpkins. Nominalists, however, deny that universals exist in things. Moreover, individual pumpkins show a good deal of variation in characteristics. How can studying them produce the systematic generalization science requires?

4.1 Ockham on Scientific Universality

Ockham considers nominalism an advantage rather than a liability when it comes to science. Aristotelian realists, he points out, are forced to the position that the things scientists study exist in two ways. In so far as we can observe and experiment on them, they are particular and concrete; in so far as they provide a unifying object for science, they are universal and abstract. Ockham impatiently concludes that this line of reasoning is "completely worthless because I could just as easily say that a human being considered in one way is an ass, in another, is an ox, and in a third, is a she-goat." [OPh IV 13, B14]

Yet Ockham wholeheartedly agrees with Aristotle that "Science is of the universal." How can this be?

Recall that Ockham never says universals do not exist at all—what he says is that universals do not exist *outside the mind.* For Ockham, the object of scientific study, and the referent of scientific universalizing statements, are universal concepts. On his view, zoologists directly perceive (i.e., have sensory/intuitive cognitions of) particular animals, and this is what causes them to form general concepts, and to make universal statements reflecting these general concepts; but, what they study and have knowledge of is the concepts and statements themselves. Ockham writes,

> The science of nature is neither about the things that are born and die, nor about natural substances, nor about the things we see moving around, for none of these things is subject or predicate in any conclusion known by natural science. Properly speaking, the science of nature is about intentions of the mind that are common to such things, and that stand precisely for such things in many statements. [OPh IV 11; B11]

Here and elsewhere Ockham uses the term "intention" for concepts in order to stress their mind-dependent status.

In Ockham's view, abstractive cognition explains the universality of science. When you have the belief that pumpkins in general turn orange, this belief is relevant not only to the pumpkins you have experienced. It is relevant to all pumpkins, including those you have not yet experienced and those you will never experience. The reason is that it is about the concept in your mind that is equally applicable to all pumpkins. In fact, you can know about a type without ever experiencing instances of it at all. Once you understand what it would mean for something to be a cat, you can know that cats beget kittens. Once you understand what it would mean for something to be a black hole, you can theorize about how black holes behave. Scientists can know universals whether or not they have perceived the relevant individuals, though the science is much more reliable when the knowledge is derived from perceptions.

4.2 Aristotle's Rationalism

Aristotle thought that the task of the scientist is to infer facts about particular individuals from their universal essences. Thus, for him, scientific reasoning consists principally in *deductive* arguments. One starts with general premises and, from these, one deduces specific conclusions. Here is an example of such a scientific syllogism:

(1) A human being is a rational animal;

(2) Margaret is a human being;

Therefore, (3) Margaret is a rational animal.

This reasoning is clearly valid, but where does Premise (1) come from? Most medieval Aristotelians interpreted Aristotle as saying that these "first principles" are necessary and self-evident. Perceiving Margaret *qua* individual will not yield any first principles. But perceiving her *qua* human will. The intellect somehow comes to understand universal *humanness* by encountering it as it inheres in her. This understanding of *humanness* itself becomes the content of Premise (1).

Although this is a kind of empiricism about the origin of concepts, it is also strongly rationalistic about the foundations of scientific belief. It makes science very substantially *a-priori*: a matter of reasoning rather than experiment and observation.

Ockham tries to be as Aristotelian as possible about science. In several places throughout his work, he appears to endorse Aristotle's rationalist definition, according to which science is evident knowledge of necessary truths deduced from a syllogism. [E.g., OPh IV 6] Ockham's conception of necessity, however, qualifies The Philosopher's view in ways that make it less and less rationalist.

4.3 Ockham on Necessity

Ockham took the logic of general statements to have *existential import*; that is, they are false if their terms do not refer to existing things. In modern logical terms, Ockham would symbolize, "An S is a P" or "All Ss are Ps" as:

$$(x)(Sx \supset Px) \ \& \ (\exists x)(Sx \ \& \ Px)$$

Since the existence of every particular individual is contingent, the statements about them, which assert the existence of one or more of them, are too. He writes,

> It is evident that, although this contradicts what Aristotle says, no statement concerning those things that signify corruptible things in an affirmative, present, and categorical way is able to be the principle or the conclusion of a demonstration. All such statements are contingent. [OPh I 512-513]

This makes Premise (1) of the Margaret syllogism contingent rather than necessary.

Ockham is willing to allow as necessary, and as knowable a-priori, what he calls "statements that contain a condition or a possibility." The conditional version of Premise (1) is: "*If* there is a human being, *then* he or she is a rational animal." In modern logical terms, this would be symbolized as:

$$(x)(Sx \supset Px)$$

This statement does not carry existential import. Ockham tries to show that this conditional construal of necessity is sufficient to satisfy the definition of science.

Ockham cannot make heads or tails of the idea that we "encounter the universal" when we "perceive a thing *qua* member of its species." For him, the necessity of scientific generalizations derives from the fact that their subject matter is really concepts, not things. The truth of the Premise (1) generalization, then, is primarily a matter of the nature of the concepts *human being* and *rational animal*. The statement is only derivatively applicable to external things—if anything in the world happens to fit this concept.

Suppose, as Aristotle did, that one general and necessary truth of science is that human beings are rational animals. (It should be noted that Ockham was not himself sure of this conception of our species. He considers characterizing human beings as the *risible* animal—those animals that are capable of laughing!)

We should understand this alleged truth as saying that the concept *human* involves the concept *rational animal*. A statement that derives its necessity from this sort of conceptual involvement is what later philosophers have called *analytic*.

Another way of putting this account of necessity is to concentrate not on the concepts but on the words that express them. The sentence "All human beings are rational animals" would be taken to express a necessary truth, then, because the definition of the word "human" includes "rational animal." The sentence is necessary because it is true by definition.

4.4 Natures

Aristotle, of course, had meant much more by necessity than Ockham was willing to allow. On Aristotle's view, the necessity in science comes, not from definitional truths, but from natural necessity in the world. What is natural necessity? According to realists like Aristotle, the fact that Margaret lives in Savannah is contingent, but the fact that Margaret is a rational animal is necessary. This means that were Margaret to move to Charleston, she would still be Margaret, but were she to lose her rationality, she would stop being herself—Margaret would be no more. *She* cannot be other than rational. The realist position is that classifications made on the basis of natural necessity are scientific, while contingent, sometimes called "accidental," classifications are not.

Ockham accepts the idea that science is meant to discover the true natures or "essences" of things, but puts his own nominalist spin on it. First, he denies that these essences are universals. He writes,

> Properly speaking, no universal belongs to the essence of any substance, for every universal is an intention of the mind or a conventional sign and nothing of either sort can belong to the essence of substance. Consequently, no genus, nor any species, nor any other universal belongs to the essence of any substance. [OPh I 59; L 86]

For Ockham, universals are concepts and words that are not to be identified with the essence of a thing.

Second, Ockham tells us what the essence of a thing is to be identified with. The essence of a thing is nothing other than its existence. The Divine Annihilation Principle is useful for establishing this point. Ockham writes,

> If existence and essence were two things rather than one, then no contradiction would be involved if God preserved the essence of a thing in the world without its existence, or vice versa, its existence without its essence. But each of these things is impossible. We have to say, therefore, that essence and existence are not two things. On the contrary, the words "existent" and "essence" signify one and the same thing. [OPh I 553-4; B 93]

Whereas virtually all of his contemporaries conceived of essence as something that precedes and informs the existence of a thing, Ockham refuses to recognize the distinction. So nothing more is necessary for finding out Margaret's essence than perceiving Margaret. But on what basis can we distinguish which of Margaret's characteristics are part of her nature, and which are merely contingent?

Ockham insists that natural necessity is nothing but a matter of how we conceptualize things. Insofar as we conceptualize Margaret as human, we would take it as necessary (by definition) that she be a rational animal (assuming that we follow Aristotle's definition). On the other hand, insofar as we conceptualize her as Savannah-resident, we would take it as necessary that she not move to Charleston. Moreover, deduction will not tell us which is the correctly scientific way to conceptualize her. For that, we have to reason empirically, using *induction*.

4.5 Induction

Ockham faces a special problem explaining where scientific generalizations come from. He cannot give Plato's answer (that we have innate knowledge of the universal forms) or Aristotle's (that we perceive the universal forms in things), because he does not believe in universal forms.

Instead, Ockham maintains that scientific generalizations arise through intuitive cognitions of a number of particular individuals. This is induction. An inductive argument derives a general truth from similar instances. Providing an example of how this process might work, Ockham writes,

> Suppose you see that a man who has a fever gets his health back when he consumes a certain herb. After eliminating all other possible causes of this cure, you know evidently that the herb was the cause. This is a single experiment of a singular thing. Nevertheless, you know that every individual of the same kind has an effect of the same kind for someone in an equally disposed condition. Hence, you evidently know the statement, "Every herb of species *x* cures fever." [OTh I 87]

Ockham's formula, "every individual of the same kind has an effect of the same kind" is a *Principle of Induction* and it enables him to think of scientific reasoning on Aristotle's syllogistic model.

Deductive reasoning is preferable because you know that, if the premises are true, then the conclusion has to be true. Inductive reasoning, in contrast, allows a false conclusion even when the premises are true. Take the following example of inductive reasoning:

(1) Jingleberry 1 cures fever.

(2) Jingleberry 2 cures fever.

(3) Jingleberry 3 cures fever.

Therefore, (4) Every jingleberry will cure fever.

This argument is not valid. It leaves us with the uncertainty that scientists despise. Nevertheless, using a Principle of Induction we can turn the same line of reasoning into a deductive syllogism:

(1) This jingleberry cures fever.

(2) Every individual of the same kind has an effect of the same kind.

Therefore, (3) Every jingleberry will cure fever.

This argument is valid, and therefore more suitable for scientific thinking.

But, is the argument sound? In particular, is Premise (2) true? Ockham treats it as a necessary truth. After all, the statement, "Every individual of the same kind has an effect of the same kind" is analytic insofar as "same kind" is defined in terms of "same effects."

Nor is this an empty gesture in Aristotle's direction. A central tenet of Ockham's metaphysics is the thesis that individuals are to be seen, fundamentally, as collections of powers. Powers are the characteristics basic to the construction of kinds. Similarity of (causal) power, then, must constitute the similarity on which successful science constructs its kinds.

So, if you have your kinds sorted out correctly, then your syllogism will be sound. Ockham writes,

> What Aristotle means to say is that, in a demonstration, you can never get a necessary conclusion from a contingent premise. Nonetheless, if you have evident knowledge of some contingent thing and knowledge of one necessary truth . . . then the conclusion they produce will be evidently known. For the necessary conclusion deduced from a contingent premise that is evidently known is known evidently, as long as the conclusion formally follows. The reasoning, "This herb heals, therefore, every herb of the same species heals" is an example of a formal inference. [OTh I 91]

The conclusion of the second jingleberry argument is guaranteed to be true if all those things we call "jingleberries" are, in fact, of the same kind.

But suppose you pick up an individual bit of herb that looks just like the bit of herb that cured the fever. Are you entitled to conclude that it will cure fever? Only insofar as you can be sure that it is of the same kind. Sameness of kind, however, is defined in terms of sameness of effects. So, this herb can indeed still fail to cure fever insofar as it can prove to be a different kind of thing. Imagine that only jingleberries growing on the north side of the hill cure fever, and only north-sided jingleberries have been examined. The conclusion would not follow for a south-side jingleberry because it is not of the same relevant kind. So, although it is necessary that all things of a kind work the same way, it is never necessary that a given individual is a thing of a given kind.

Ockham pondered a more theologically flavored example of this failure. Suppose God suspended his usual conserving power with respect to a formerly curative sample of jingleberry, and thereby left it impotent, or perhaps supplied it with the power to poison instead. This is a case of supernatural intervention, but the more general point is that it is an entirely contingent matter whether individuals live up to the requirements for membership in the relevant kind. Often they do, but sometimes they do not. When that happens, we do not distrust the Principle of Induction. Rather, we conclude we need to reconceptualize the individuals—to sort them into more scientifically adequate kinds.

4.6 Justification of Scientific Belief

Many of Ockham's contemporaries were outraged by his treatment of scientific generalization. They thought his view would make real science impossible. Their argument, in effect, was this. Zoologists predict how this rabbit will behave on the basis of the past behavior of other rabbits. If these animals are not essentially identical, then this inference is unjustified. On the other hand, if we suppose that rabbits share a universal common nature, then we can be sure that they must all behave the same. Our experience of the ways particular rabbits work would give us knowledge of how they all *have* to work, knowledge of underlying laws. In rejecting common natures and the natural necessity they guarantee, Ockham leaves himself without a justification for scientific belief.

The only response available to Ockham is to concede that inferences about particular cases are fallible. This allies Ockham firmly with a modern view of scientific knowledge. Notice that the rationalist/ realist does not argue that, if rabbits are not essentially identical, then inductive conclusions about them will be *false*. On the contrary, someone might still make a correct prediction on the basis of a similarity (as opposed to strict identity of the universal). Rather, the concern is that the inference will not *necessarily* be true. Sometimes, despite the fact that a great deal of very good inductive evidence has been collected in exactly the right way, the universal conclusion inductively inferred turns out false. Sometimes, it will be true everywhere, for a very long time, and then suddenly counter-instances will turn up.

Although scientists often make incorrect predictions, they would prefer to believe that, when they are wrong, they are wrong because they are lacking information about some factor that made the new case different. Suppose that extended scientific observation shows that rabbits prefer carrots to cabbage. Then, one day, a rabbit appears who prefers cabbage. What is the difference in this one? Is it that she, but none of the others observed previously, is pregnant, rabid, brain damaged? The assumption is that all members of a species must be essentially identical (in some designated respects), so external factors must always be responsible for variation in their behavior. On this view, someone who had perfect knowledge of essences plus external factors would have perfect knowledge of the future. This is a scientist's dream come true.

Ockham thinks it is only fair to admit, however, that this dream can never be a reality. So far as he can see, the only kind of knowledge that is perfect is evident intuitive cognition: the perception you have of an individual when you are in its presence, and are unobstructed from receiving information from it. Because every rabbit has its own nature, the only way to be sure it behaves in a way exactly similar to other rabbits is to witness its behavior directly. Not even God can predict what Thumper will do tomorrow by calculating the results of a universal rabbit nature plus external factors.

4.7 Aristotle's Four Causes

The Aristotelian view of science gives a strong place to teleological thinking. The word "teleology" comes from the Greek word for "purpose." Teleological thinking explains things by the purpose that they serve, by their end or goal.

Aristotle thought that all of reality could be explained in virtue of four *causes*. The word "cause" here is misleading. We might think of them as four sorts of explanation. Suppose we come across a cabin in the woods. A complete explanation of it involves four components:

> *Material cause*: the matter on which the form is imposed. The material cause of the cabin is wood.
>
> *Formal cause*: the form imposed on the matter. The formal cause of the cabin is its shape.
>
> *Efficient cause*: that which initiates the process of change. The efficient cause of the cabin is its builder.

Final cause: the purpose for which the object came into existence, its goal. The final cause of the cabin is to provide shel-
ter.

Even clueless aliens might understand the cabin's existence given this
fourfold explanation. Aristotle's goal was to explain everything in nature according to this model. The final cause explanation is the teleological one.

Today we find it decidedly odd to give final cause explanations in
the physical sciences. As physical science has come to rely on efficient
cause as the primary form of explanation, final cause explanation has
dropped out. Why do rivers run downhill to the sea? It is not because
they have a goal to reach. It is just because gravity exerts a push on
everything. End of story.

But not for Aristotle. He thought that final causality was a necessary ingredient in any complete explanation. The reason is that the
other sorts of explanation leave you wondering why—why things do
what they do; why there exists this particular thing rather than that;
why there exists something rather than nothing at all. Aristotle wanted
an explanation to end all explanations, so he worked up a teleology for
nature as a whole. He seems to have had in mind an aesthetic ideal of
health and beauty. The cosmos attempts to achieve its aim, he writes,
"like a doctor doctoring himself." [Physics, II]

Ockham was very taken with the first three of Aristotle's four
causes. Nevertheless, he thought that Aristotle was mistaken to consider "final causality" a cause. He writes,

> If I accepted no authority, I would claim that it cannot be
> proved either from statements known in themselves or from
> experience that every effect has a final cause. [OTh IX; Q
> 246]

> Someone who is just following natural reason would claim
> that the question "Why?" is inappropriate in the case of natu-
> ral actions. For he would maintain that it is no real question to
> ask something like, "For what reason is fire generated?" [OTh
> IX 299; Q 249]

Ockham is even more reluctant than usual to quarrel openly with the
authority of The Philosopher in this case, since the Church had its own
theological reasons for endorsing Aristotle's teleology.

There are two areas in which contemporary thought accepts
something like final-cause explanation, and Ockham deals interestingly
with both.

The first is in the explanation of human action. Ockham accepts the obvious truth that a person's goals are relevant when explaining that person's actions. Nevertheless, he resists the idea that somehow our goals in the future pull us toward them in the present, with the cause coming well after its supposed effect. For Ockham, explaining actions by citing their goals merely serves to specify the current motivation of the people who are acting. Thus when Gwendolyn runs down the street because she wants to arrive at the movie downtown on time fifteen minutes from now, it is not her future arrival that is causing her running, it is her current desire to get there fifteen minutes from now. Ockham remarks that even in the explanation of human action, final causes are "causes" only in an extended, metaphorical sense of the word. [OTh VIII 113-4]

The second area is "functional" thinking in biology: we speak of the "purpose" of the pancreas, for example. In general, mechanistic explanation, free of teleology, supplanted Aristotelian thought in the physical sciences fairly soon after Ockham. In the life sciences, however, final causes persisted well into the nineteenth century. How else to explain why woodpeckers develop such a strong sharp bill, other than by citing the purpose that this bill serves for the woodpecker and for nature as a whole?

With the arrival of Charles Darwin (1809-1882), all this changed, and science, at last, was able to explain apparently purposeful phenomena in organisms through the mechanisms of natural selection. The basic idea behind Darwin's revolution was much older, however, having been introduced by Empedocles (born early fifth century B.C.), reported by Aristotle, and seriously considered by Ockham. Ockham provides an extended treatment of the subject. He writes,

> The necessity of nature brings it about that the parts in some animals are conveniently arranged for the health of the whole. For example, the front teeth are sharp and apt for dividing food and the molars are flat and apt for mashing food. The front teeth would become sharp and the back would become flat, however, even if they were not apt for these uses, and thus they did not come into being *because of* such uses. Just as it is with these parts of animals, so also it is with the other parts of the animals that would come to be such from the necessity of matter, although no uses were intended. Consequently, these parts do not exist *because of* such uses. Rather, when they come to be, then the animals survive. The reason is this: from such a disposition of parts the health of the animal

comes about by chance. These parts become apt for conserving the animal by chance. Indeed, they would equally come to be as they are from the necessity of nature even though such a disposition would not be convenient for the health of the animal. [OPh IV 370-371]

Whereas Aristotle had rejected Empedocles's idea, Ockham rejected Aristotle's rejection, finding The Philosopher's counterarguments "inconclusive." In so doing, he provides direction for better things to come.

It is clear overall that Ockham was a key figure in questioning teleological thinking in science. This development, together with the empiricist turn, are arguably the most important events in the history of science. Only after faith in Aristotelian science was shaken could the scientific revolution of the Renaissance begin.

5
Meaning and Reference

Despite the broad scope of his work, Ockham thought of himself first and foremost as a logician. Whereas Thomas Aquinas's crowning achievement was a *Summa Theologiae* ("Summary of Theology"), Ockham's was a *Summa Logicae* ("Summary of Logic"). The reason is that Ockham's razoring innovations really were a matter of logic, construed broadly as philosophy of language. Think about Ockham's attack on hypostatization, which we have seen at work a number of times. The idea in each case is to show that the fact that we can talk about something (e.g., *greenness*) does not mean it really exists. The general logical point is that you do not need to posit abstract referents to make sense of abstract terms.

Through his experience as a teacher and a debater in the university community, Ockham became convinced that a great number of hopeless confusions arise when philosophers fail to understand how language works. So he elaborated a whole system of logic that supports the thesis that universals do not exist outside the mind.

5.1 Behaviorism versus Mentalism

Suppose you are observing a construction site. One carpenter says, "slab" and another carpenter picks up a slab and carries it over. An obvious way to think about what is going on here is to suppose that the first carpenter had something in mind when she said what she did, perhaps the particular slab the second carpenter brought over. In some way, the first carpenter's word was *about* the slab the other one brought. There was something the first carpenter thought that somehow connected with the slab. When she said, "slab," she meant slab.

The idea that words mean what they do because they stand for thoughts that connect with the world may seem like common sense. Through the years, however, philosophers have found it very difficult to explain the relation between language and the world. Ludwig Wittgenstein (1889-1951) went so far as to deny that there is any such connection. He argues that language is a system of behavior much like a game. In Monopoly, when you pass go, you get $200. Likewise, when the carpenter says "slab," she gets a slab. We do not need to suppose that "slab" *means* slab any more than passing go *means* $200. It is just an arbitrary rule. Wittgenstein's view is a kind of *behaviorism*: the meaning of language is explained by the part it plays in societal behavior.

Ockham was one of the many philosophers throughout history who tried to elaborate an alternative to behaviorism. His view, sometimes called *mentalism* about meaning, holds that meaning is explained by the mental state of the language user.

5.2 Natural Signification

For Ockham, language signifies things. The word "mountain" signifies mountains. How and why does it do this? It seems obvious that this happens because the speaker means mountain when that speaker says the word. The speaker must have some mental act, according to Ockham; he must believe or desire or hope *about* mountains. When someone else hears (or reads) that word, communication takes place because that other person comes to think (believe, or desire, or intend to do something, etc.) about mountains too.

But, what is involved in thinking about (believing something about, hoping for, etc.) mountains? Some philosophers have argued that our thoughts are mental pictures. So your thought for mountain means mountain because it literally resembles a mountain—much as the picture in a passport resembles its bearer. Wittgenstein and Ockham both flirted with this view early in their careers. The problem with it is that it goes with a representationalist epistemology, which we have already seen good reasons for avoiding. Ockham opted instead for what is today called a *causal theory of reference*, and it is designed to compliment his direct realist epistemology. Your word "mountain" means mountain because the thought you think when you say it or write it is caused by the mountain you perceived.

According to Ockham, it is a consequence of the way you are naturally constituted that things have the power to cause certain mental events in you. This then is *natural signification*. Speakers of different

37

languages have similar natural constitutions, and respond to mountains with the same kind of mental event. Nevertheless, they use different public language words: "mountain" or "*Berg*" or "*montagne.*" This shows that public language has only *artificial signification*: human beings are taught to associate mountain-words with mountain-thoughts.

Ockham provides an analogy for understanding his causal account of signification. Suppose there is a pub owner who has just received his monthly shipment of wine. He needs to communicate to the townspeople that the wine has arrived. So, after transferring the wine from barrels to bottles, he hangs the empty barrel hoops outside the pub. His sign means "Wine's here!" Note that the arrival of the wine *causes* the proliferation of empty barrel hoops, it does not *resemble* them. Likewise, perceiving a mountain causes a neuron to fire in a certain way. If you could see the perceiver's neuron firing, you could infer the cause, even though that firing does not resemble a mountain. Since we cannot see into one another's minds, we associate the firing with a vocal sound or written shape (we hang the hoop outside). This sound or shape signifies, not the firing, but the mountain that caused it. [OPh I 9; L 50]

5.3 Mentalese

The epistemological side of this story, how the human mind acquires thoughts about things, is something we have already discussed. Ockham accepted the standard late medieval view that human beings are born blank slates and that the things we encounter in the world cause thoughts of themselves in us. These thoughts begin as absolutely specific intuitive cognitions of individuals. After exposure to many similar individuals, we generate a single abstract concept that applies equally to each of them (universals).

There is also a logical story to be told, however, about how we string these concepts together. We do not just think mountain. We believe or hope or assert or deny something about mountains: that this is a mountain, that this mountain is taller than that one, and so on. How do we account for all the elements of these thoughts?

Medieval logicians distinguished two basically different sorts of words in language:

> *Categorematic signs,* like "mountain" and "tall," signify things and characteristics. They fill the place of subjects and predicates in sentences.

> *Syncategorematic signs,* like "all," "is," and "not," modify subjects and predicates in various ways.

Today we would say that categorematic signs function *semantically* (content, meaning) while syncategorematic signs function syntactically (form, structure). To think and to speak is to combine categorematic terms with syncategorematic terms. On Ockham's view, pronouncing the categorematic term "slab" is not really language at all unless it is understood as elliptical for something like "Will you please bring me a slab?" which includes the requisite syncategorematic elements.

Whereas categorematic words get their meaning because we associate them with empirically experienced objects, syncategorematic words get their meaning because we associate them with logical functions. They do not have any natural signification of their own. As Ockham explains,

> This is just as in arithmetic. Taken all by itself, zero does not signify anything, but adding another number makes it signify. Likewise, a syncategorematic term does not signify anything, properly speaking. Nevertheless, adding another term makes it signify something or stand for something in a determinate manner or fulfill some other function with respect to the categorematic term. [OPh I 15; L 55]

Syncategorematic terms are more like tools than signs. The word "all" universalizes, the word "not" negates, the word "is" identifies, etc. Give these tools some concepts to operate on and you have speech.

The analogy between the elements and principles of combination that constitute public language and those that constitute thought allows us to think of thought as a sort of language-use. Thinking does not use the words of public language, however. In order to be able to express a thought in a public language, one has to learn that language. And the process of learning a language involves the association of bits of that language with bits of thought. This implies that one must already be capable of thinking in order to learn the language. Ockham concluded that the language of thinking must be prior to, and possible without, public language. Contemporary philosophers who agree, such as Noam Chomsky (1928-), sometimes call the language of the mind "*Mentalese.*"

Ockham uses the idea of Mentalese to explain how angels communicate. They have no mouths for speaking, ears for listening, hands for writing, or eyes for reading; so, they cannot use public language. Ockham writes,

> An angel, in speaking to another angel, does nothing other than cause within himself an act of thinking about something,

an act of thinking that, as an object, effectively causes within the "listening" angel an act of thinking about that act of thinking. And so, as a result, this, in some way, causes within the "listening" angel an act of thinking about the object of the first act of thinking. [OTh IX 37-8; Q 35-6]

As usual, we need not believe in angels to appreciate Ockham's philosophical point, which is that we can conceive of acts of thinking, and therefore of acts of communication, without the aid of external behavior. As long as you have the requisite categorematic and syncategorematic elements, combined in the right way, you have language. If you can get another mind to notice these elements, you have communication.

5.4 Ockham's Innatism

Ockham is an *innatist* about language: he thinks that the basic structure of public language is also the structure of Mentalese, and that this structure is innate. How does this fit with his claim that human beings are born blank slates?

Ockham does not hold that human beings are born with predesignated mental symbols or pictures to which conventional public-language words can later be assigned; we have to wait until we perceive real things before we acquire the corresponding thoughts. We do come with the potential to have internal "words" caused in us by external stimuli, but this is not really any sort of innate structure. A blank chalkboard has the potential for markings to occur on it, as a function of the motions of an external piece of chalk, but this does not show that those symbols are somehow already in the chalkboard.

Rather, what we are born with are the *syncategorematica*, the mental equipment that enables us to manipulate the thoughts that we are about to acquire. In contemporary versions of innatism, it is sometimes said that our minds are built with a "blank grammar." Ockham would be averse to characterizing mental equipment in such a way that it sounds like a thing; for him, syncategorematica are linguistic powers.

Think of this innate power as a set of variously shaped boxes connected by levers, chains, cranks, and conveyer belts. The boxes stand for our mental variables for nouns, verbs, adjectives, and adverbs, which we fill with impressions as we go through life. Each type of box is different; for example, noun boxes come with instructions for singular or plural, verb boxes for past, present, or future tense, adjective boxes for hooking up with nouns, and adverbs for comparative degree. The machinery moving these boxes around stands both for connectives

like "the," "and," "if," "but," etc., as well as for incomplete preposi-
tions such as "on the ____," "under the ____," etc., which are completed in connection with the noun boxes.

This is a simplistic picture, of course, and mental language is
surely much more powerful. Consider the fact that Chinese has no word
for "the" and no tense-modifiers for verbs. When we translate Chinese
into English we insert "the" and all of the tenses. Chinese is not defec-
tive; it manages to convey equivalent grammatical concepts in its own
economical ways. The point is that Mentalese is probably more economical than any spoken language (which is why most people can think
much faster than they speak or write). It contains only the absolutely
bare-bones common denominator of all human language, whatever that
may be.

Ockham spends some time thinking about which elements of conventional languages would be unnecessary in mental language. His
guiding principle seems to be that we can safely razor anything that is
synonymous. If "bachelor" and "unmarried man" mean exactly the
same thing, then there will be just one mental word for them. These two
words probably do not mean exactly the same thing because of different connotations. But consider the following two sentences:

Socrates runs.

Socrates is running.

Do they correspond to just one mental sentence or two? Ockham re-
plies,

> There is no need to posit a plurality for such sentences in the
> mind, since a verb is always equivalent in signification to, and
> synonymous with, the participle of the verb taken together
> with the verb "is." Synonymous names were instituted, not be-
> cause of any requirement of signification, but only for the sake
> of embellishing speech. For, whatever is signified and ex-
> pressed by each of several synonymous names could ade-
> quately be expressed by one of them. This is why there is no
> plurality of concepts corresponding to the several synonymous
> names. [OTh IX 512-513; Q 428]

Ockham's strategy here is, as usual, simplicity. We should postulate
only those explanatory elements that are necessary.

41

5.5 Supposition

Consider the word "horse." The meaning of this word comes from its association with a general concept, and it can be applied to any of the horses you have seen, as well as to any you have not. The word has meaning all by itself, but it has *reference* only when used as a term within a sentence. Medievals used the word "*suppositio*" for reference because it means "standing-for." We should examine Ockham's three-fold account of supposition because it provided critical support for his nominalism.

PERSONAL SUPPOSITION

According to Ockham, in the sentence, "Frenchy is a horse," the term "horse" refers to the same thing that the term "Frenchy" does. *That* (pointing to Frenchy) is what "Frenchy" means. This is the most basic form of referring and Ockham called it *personal supposition.* The same goes for the sentence, "My horses are in the field." Here, the term "horses" stands for Frenchy, Dobbin, and Prince. (It should be noted that there are historical reasons why Ockham called this sort of supposition "personal"; it does not mean that you can refer in this way only to persons.)

By generalizing our acquired concepts through abstractive cognition we are able to signify things in their absence and things that we have never perceived. In the sentence, "Horses are four-legged," the term "horses" personally supposits many more horses than you have actually perceived. What we are saying is more explicitly paraphrased as, "All horses are four-legged." Ockham thought of this sentence as being equivalent to a long conjunction:

Frenchy is four-legged and Dobbin is four-legged and . . . .

Adding the syncategorematic terms "all," "some," "none," etc., fixes the reference in many different ways, so there are many different types of personal supposition.

MATERIAL SUPPOSITION

Suppose someone says the following sentence to you: "Horse has five letters." What she has said is true. Nevertheless, none of the things the word "horse" signifies has five letters. The speaker has used a spoken word to stand for a written word. She is not referring to any horse; she is referring to the word, "horse."

When the name of a word occurs in writing, we use quotation marks to distinguish it, and nowadays we say that such a word is being *mentioned* rather than *used*. Compare:

I put a piece of tape on the chalkboard.

I put "a piece of tape" on the chalkboard.

The second sentence refers to the words you wrote. The medievals called cases in which spoken and written words are used to refer to themselves cases of *material supposition*. (Note, again, that this type of reference is not meant to be restricted to material objects.)

SIMPLE SUPPOSITION

Finally, consider the following true sentence: "A horse is a kind of animal." What does "horse" stand for here? It does not stand for Frenchy, who is an animal, not a *kind* of animal. It does not stand for each of Frenchy and Dobbin and Prince, or even for the set of all horses in the universe, because none of them is a *kind* of animal. Nor does the notion of material supposition help. The term "horse" does not stand for a word because no word is a kind of animal.

This sentence is clearly meaningful and true. How are we to explain its reference? Ockham's answer is that this is a case in which a written word stands for a mental word. He writes,

> *Simple supposition* occurs when a term stands for an intention of the mind and is not functioning significatively. For example, in *"Human being* is a species," the term "human being" stands for an intention of the mind. For it is this intention that is the species. [OPh I 196; L 190]

The idea is that, although the term "human being" normally stands for Hypatia and Heraclitus and Hypocrates, and so on, the term "human being" can stand for the mental concept that signifies all these objects while not standing for any of them at all.

Note how simple supposition solves the problem of reference for the sentence, "A horse is a kind of animal." We all agree that this sentence is true. Ockham would count this sentence as true if and only if the subject term ("horse") and the predicate term ("kind of animal") stood for a single thing, the same single thing. What single thing does "a kind of animal" stand for? Ockham's view of universals makes kind-terms such as this one stand for concepts. So this sentence is true provided that the subject term "horse" also stands for a concept.

Medieval realists, who originally named this type of supposition "simple," were thinking that it was a case in which you refer to the universal form of a thing alone without also referring to any individual instances of it. They thought of the word "horse" as primarily signifying the universal form *horseness*. For them, therefore, simple supposition was a case of suppositing significatively, and personal supposition, in which one refers to instances, was not. Ockham turns this realist analysis upside down. If we understand cases of personal supposition as signifying in a primary way, then simple (and material) supposition can be understood as non-significative, that is, as not referring to external objects in the usual primary way. *Voila*, the nominalist theory of reference: when you are talking universal-talk, you are not referring to anything outside the mind.

5.6 Absolute and Connotative Terms

Categorematic terms refer to things in the world, and, on Ockham's view, the only things there are in the world are particular substances and particular qualities. This implies that every categorematic term refers either to a particular substance or to a particular quality. A human being is a particular substance and happy is a particular quality. Hence, it is not hard to see how we come to have terms for these things.

Consider the term "parent," however. Both "human being" and "parent" refer to people, but it appears that there is a difference in the way these two terms refer. Something is a human being just because of the way it is, but for something to be a parent, things have to be true of the world outside that person: someone else has to exist who is that person's offspring. The term "parent," in a way, refers to two things.

Clearly, any philosophy of language needs a mechanism for handling this distinction. Ockham's mechanism, connotation, turns out to play a key role in the nominalist solution to a wide variety of logical difficulties.

Ockham distinguishes two different types of categorematic terms:

> *Absolute terms*, like "human being" and "happy" signify things in the world directly.

> *Connotative terms* signify one thing directly and another thing indirectly.

The term "parent" signifies a human being directly, and others begotten by him or her indirectly.

Ockham asserts that the difference between concepts like *human being* and *parent* lies in the definition. When the term *human being* is defined as "corporeal-sensory-intellective substance," it expresses a real essence. This is to say that it describes the nature of the thing that causes the concept *human being* in the first place. Every individual human being naturally signifies or calls to mind a thought amounting to *corporeal-sensory-intellective-substance*. So a real-essence definition puts into words the base content of the perception of a human being. And because we assume that things really are what we, at our best, perceive them to be, the real-essence definition is said to express the "what" of the thing. The definition of *parent*, in contrast, would be something like "human being who has begotten others." It *denotes* a human being while *connoting* a relation to other human beings. Because of the added connotation, it cannot be said to describe the content of your perception of Dad. It expresses what Ockham calls a *nominal essence*. He writes,

> Properly speaking, only absolute names, that is, concepts signifying things composed of matter and form, have definitions expressing real essence. Some examples of this sort of name are "human being," "lion," and "goat." Connotative and relative names, on the other hand, which signify one thing directly and another thing indirectly, have definitions expressing nominal essence. Some examples of this sort of name are "white," "hot," "parent," and "child." [OPh IX 554; Q 463-4]

For Ockham, connotative names are basically relative names: they indicate a relation between things.

We can see why Ockham counted *being a human* metaphysically basic and *being a parent* relational. When a parcel of matter becomes a human, or stops (at death), there is a real change in it. If you are male, however, you can become a parent without a direct change in you. When your partner gives birth, and your first-born child appears, you become a parent, even at some distance away and even if you are not aware of it. Being a parent is being related in a certain way to something else, and the coming-to-existence of that something else is, under certain circumstances, sufficient to establish that relation. Somebody might find out all the real-essence facts about you while remaining ignorant that you are a parent.

The distinction between absolute and connotative terms implies a difference in the origin of the concepts connected to these terms. When we receive a concept directly through intuitive cognition, we perceive the individual qualities inherent in the substance. Absolute terms, then, which concern substance and qualities, are capable of what contemporary philosophers call *ostensive definition*: you find out what they mean by looking at what someone is pointing at. But you can observe parents pointed out to you as long as you like and still not come up with the concept. This is because *parenthood* is neither a substance nor a quality but a relation.

If the concept *parenthood* does not come from a substance or quality out there in the world, then where does it come from? In Ockham's view, it comes from the understanding. There are qualities in the parent (like having certain DNA) and qualities in the child (like having exactly similar DNA) which imply a certain familial categorization. It is unnecessary to suppose that there is some abstract entity connecting the two individuals. Ockham insists that it is absurd to suppose that relations are real "little things" stretching between substances. Like universals, relations are nothing but concepts in the mind concerning substances. [See Quod 6.16.]

5.7 Numbers

It is not surprising to see Ockham razoring relations in much the same way that he razored universals. What is more surprising is the way in which this led him to razor numbers as well. Ockham argued long and hard that quantity is nothing but a concept in the mind about individual substances. This is striking considering that even W.V. Quine (1908-), a prominent twentieth-century nominalist, holds that mathematics requires positing the existence of numbers in the form of sets.

It is also striking considering that Ockham had to brave stringent opposition in order to make his case. As a matter of fact, Ockham's refusal to recognize the existence of quantity involved him in the heresy investigation for which he was called away from Oxford. It deserves a brief mention here.

Ockham was investigated for heresy concerning his teaching on transubstantiation. Transubstantiation is the miracle that is supposed to happen during the Catholic Eucharist when bread and wine is changed into the body and blood of Christ.

The medievals devoted a lot of energy to making sense of this miracle. According to the standard view, qualities like the white of the bread inhere in the quantity of the bread, which remains when the substance of the bread is replaced by the substance of Christ. Ockham, however, thought that to say "a quantity of bread remains" is simply to say that the substance of the bread remains. What else is a quantity of bread if not the bread itself? Yet, at the same time, it would be blasphemous to assert that when the substance of the bread disappears, the qualities of the bread come to inhere in Christ. So Ockham asserted instead that the qualities of the bread do not inhere in anything after the substance of the bread disappears. Rather, they simply subsist on their own: a white, a sweet, and a crunchy accompany the substance of Christ into the mouth of the Catholic. [See OTh X 110.]

This is the view that the Church would not accept. To Ockham, the issue was a matter of logic and physics. To the Church, it was a matter of tradition and authority. What is interesting about the conflict is that Ockham was not challenging the miraculous status of the phenomenon (the way the Protestants would in years to come). On the contrary, his version is *more* miraculous. But perhaps this is precisely what made it seem dangerous. Whereas the standard view tries to pass transubstantiation off in routine metaphysical terms, on Ockham's view, it appears utterly anomalous and bizarre, ripe for ridicule and rejection.

Nevertheless, Ockham thought he had been sufficiently accommodating. You can say that Christ becomes present, you can even say that the bread disappears, but you cannot say that a quantity of something remains if the substance of it does not. He stuck to his guns, and he got into trouble. This is why, when he comes around to asserting that quantity does not exist, he often couches his position in terms of an anonymous source.

"Some say," he writes, that the notion of connotation is sufficient to save the meaning of numerical adjectives. Something is called "one" precisely in so far as all of its parts can be said to constitute a single thing. A single thing is called "two" precisely in so far as it is considered in combination with any other single thing. As Ockham put it, all the numbers higher than one "signify the things themselves while connoting that these things do not together make for something one in itself." [OTh IV 112]

This is not an implausible suggestion. If you have a coconut on the table, you conceive of it as *one*. If you put another coconut on the table, it becomes *one-of-two*: the grouping changes your conception of the first coconut by giving it the relational property. *Two* is a nominal essence, connoting a relation between things.

5.8 Non-existent Things

Ockham holds a causal theory of reference: the concepts used in language are caused in us by the things in the world that they signify. But then, what about concepts that have no reference? We have the concept *golden mountain*, and we can speak these words meaningfully. They refer to something that could exist but does not. Worse yet, we have the concept *square circle*. It neither does nor can signify anything because a square circle (the locus of points equidistant from a given point, with four equal straight-line sides and four right angles) is an impossible object. So what are we talking about when we talk about it? In a memorable philosophical move, Alexius Meinong (1853-1920) posited a whole universe of non-existent existents to serve as the referents for such concepts.

You can bet Ockham was not about to do that. His answer to how these concepts arise and refer comes from his theory of abstractive cognition whereby concepts caused by some particular thing can be detached from that thing and used independently.

The real essence of an object is its fundamental existence. Non-existent objects cannot have real essences. When we perceive something and that thing causes a concept in our minds, we produce an ostensive definition of the concept, formed on the basis of the real essence of the thing perceived. Gold, mountains, circles, and squares thus have real-essence definitions. Non-existent objects like golden mountains and square circles, however, cannot have real-essence definitions. Their definitions are concocted by combining the real-essence definitions of their component parts. Concocted definitions of this sort are nominal-essence definitions. Ockham writes,

> Real-essence definitions include only possible and actual things, whereas nominal-essence definitions, while including possible and actual things, also extend to impossible things. Words like "vacuum," "non-being," "impossible thing," "infinite extension," "chimera," and "goat-stag" have nominal-essence definitions. To these names, there correspond certain phrases that signify the same things as the names do. [OTh IX 555-556; Q 464]

Terms with nominal-essence definitions have no personal supposition in a sentence, but they do have simple supposition: they refer to uninstantiated concepts of the mind.

It is worth mentioning in this connection that Ockham did not consider a vacuum to be an impossible object. Most of his contemporaries, following Aristotle, were convinced that "Nature abhors a vacuum." Ockham, however, points out that God could easily make a vacuum by annihilating everything (including the air) inside a house. [See Quod 1.8.] Therefore, vacuums are possible. A few centuries later, Enlightenment scientists would prove him correct.

It should be evident from this brief survey how Ockham's logic facilitates philosophical analysis. Not only did it serve his own project in parsimony, it also made a profound impact on the history of formal logic and linguistic analysis in general.

6
God

We saw in the last chapter that Ockham uses the notion of connotation for explaining language about things that do not and cannot exist. He also uses it, however, for things that exist beyond our experience.

Suppose (what seems likely) that you have never seen a platypus. The way you have learned the meaning of the term "platypus" is by looking up the definition: "a semiaquatic, egg-laying mammal of Australia and Tasmania, having a broad, flat tail, webbed feet, and a snout resembling a duck's bill." For you, at the moment, this is a nominal definition. It asks you to combine your concepts of mammals, ducks, and Australia into a single concept. This is sufficient to allow you to use the term meaningfully. You can say, for example, "I've never seen a platypus." It is also sufficient to give you the capacity for applying the term, should you happen to meet one, in all its peculiar glory. If you did, from then on, "platypus" would function as an absolute term for you with a real-essence definition.

Ockham thought that this is exactly the situation human beings are in with respect to God. He believed, or at least hoped, that human beings would one day have evident intuitive cognitions of God, face to face. Meanwhile, we live with nothing more than a nominal definition.

Despite the fact that belief in God was widely supposed to be a matter of faith, many medieval philosophers thought of theology as a kind of science. Ockham thought this was complete nonsense. In this chapter, we will see how he clarifies the concept of God and draws the line between faith and reason.

6.1 Experience of God

Gothic Europe was full of mystics. Meister Eckhart (c. 1260-1328) and Catharine of Siena (c. 1347-1380), for example, both asserted that human beings can achieve "union with the divine." Ockham, however, stands in stark contrast to such figures. Not only does he deny that human beings are capable of uniting with God, he denies that we can have any knowledge of God properly speaking. Ockham was a *fideist*: he claimed that belief in God is a matter of faith alone.

Ockham's fideism can be understood as an extension of his empiricism. All knowledge comes from experience, and we have never experienced God. He writes,

> In order to demonstrate the statement of faith that we formulate about God, what we would need for the central concept is a simple cognition of the divine nature in itself—what someone who sees God has. Nevertheless, we cannot have this kind of cognition in our present state. [OTh IX 120-1; Q 103-4]

Ockham is absolutely clear: God is not accessible to human beings.

Why did Ockham take such a hard line? As a Franciscan, he was forced to respect various reports of religious experience, like those of the saints, and those in the Bible. He was bent, however, on reinterpreting all such experiences in such a way that they involve an intermediary. He writes:

> I say that neither the divine essence, nor the divine nature, nor anything intrinsic to God, nor anything that is really God, can be known by us without something other than God being involved as object. [OTh II 402]

For example, Moses communicated with God through a burning bush. The intermediary is crucial because it makes the experience indirect, and hence, fallible. Perhaps it was in the interest of preserving the naturalism in his epistemology that Ockham was reluctant to accept the possibility of a supernatural encounter. Or perhaps his conflicts with "divinely inspired" religious leaders gave him motivation to reserve room for skepticism.

6.2 Proof of God

In addition to rejecting experience of God, Ockham also rejects inference to God's existence. He considers the famous proofs of Aquinas and Anselm (1033-1109) in detail. At their best, these proofs boil down to very similar strategies in his view. Aquinas's best proof argues that there must be a First Cause because there cannot be an infinite regress of causes for the world. Anselm's proof argues that there must be a Being than which no greater can be conceived because there cannot be an infinite regress of greatness in being. Interpreting his predecessors' proofs as infinite regress proofs, Ockham gives them some credit. Ultimately, however, he finds them inconclusive. First we should note why Ockham found infinite regress proofs acceptable and then we can see where he thought Aquinas and Anselm fell short.

Ockham would accept an infinite regress proof because he firmly maintains, following Aristotle, that there can be no such thing as an infinite quantity of objects that actually exist at the same time. This sort of infinity (what Ockham called an "extensive infinity") is a numerical concept. It has a nominal-essence definition: we concoct it in our minds by thinking of someone beginning to make a series of objects and then never stopping. In order for an imagined infinite quantity of objects actually to exist at the same time it would have to be, at least in theory, entirely countable. Yet, it is not. Counting an infinite quantity would take an infinite amount of time, and so you would never get to the end. You could only get to the end if assigning each number to each object took no time at all. But this is impossible, even for God. [See Quod 3.1.]

It may seems strange that someone who continually insists on the omnipotence of God the way Ockham does would deny that God can count an infinite number of things, especially since God is traditionally conceived as living "in eternity" where there is no time at all. Two things should be pointed out, however. First of all, Ockham does not conceive of God as living outside of time in the traditional sense entrenched by Boethius (480-523). On Ockham's view, time is nothing but the measure of change in things. [See Quod 7.5.] The only reason God is said to be "timeless" is because he does not change. Second, God's omnipotence is limited by logical possibility. Ockham's point is that an infinite quantity is just as impossible as a square circle.

So, if it were true that denying the existence of God would imply the existence of an extensive infinity, then one could not rationally deny the existence of God. But, as it turns out, this is not true. Ockham's argument against both Aquinas and Anselm is that, in each case, if they establish an existence, it bears no resemblance to the Christian God.

To begin with, Ockham points out that Aquinas will not even generate a successful infinite regress argument in so far as he conceives of the series of causes of the world as successive. It is logically possible that there be an infinite quantity of causes one after another through an infinite series of time, as long as the infinite quantity in question is not supposed to exist *all at the same time*. Secondly, even if we interpret Aquinas's argument in terms of simultaneously existing conserving causes, he fails to show that the end to the regress is God. It could be that each thing simply conserves itself. [See OTh II 354ff.]

As for Anselm, he fails to show that the Being than which no greater can be conceived is God. Ockham writes,

> There would be an infinite regress among entities if there were not something such that nothing is prior or more perfect. It does not follow from this, however, that it can be demonstrated that there is just one such. Instead, this is held only by faith. [OTh IX 3; Q 6-7]

What does Ockham have in mind when he indicates that there is no guarantee of just one greatest thing? There are two interpretations.

First, he might mean that there is no absurdity in positing a tie for best. This would be true if, for example, the Father, the Son, and the Holy Spirit are totally independent beings (contrary to the doctrine of the Trinity) and are each such that nothing is better. Some people have interpreted Ockham as saying that, although the ontological proof establishes that theism is true, it does not establish which type of theism, i.e., monotheism or polytheism, is true.

Second, he might be entertaining the possibility that the entire set of presently existing things does not constitute a single category of commensurable individuals. One can compare, for example, various pitchers' curve balls, and say that Lefty Gomez's curve balls are better than anyone else's. And one can say that last night's sunset was the best all year. But one might be at a loss to say whether last night's sunset was better or worse than Lefty Gomez's curve balls.

If each category had its best, but cross-category comparisons made no sense, there might be no divine beings at all, because there would not have to be something better than everything else. Some people take Ockham to be suggesting this more radical rejection of Anselm.

Regardless of the details of interpretation, it is clear that, on Ockham's view, the alleged proofs of the existence of God are inconclusive.

6.3 Providence

So far we have seen how Ockham denies experience and proof of God. He also had some difficulty with the traditional divine attributes. The God of the Catholic faith is all-loving, omnipotent, and omniscient.

Ockham found the first two attributes easy to make sense of. But omniscience presented a considerable challenge for him. He had no problem accounting for God's knowledge of everything that is currently happening or his memory of everything that has happened. But he did have a problem accounting for God's knowledge of the future.

Some theologians think God's foreknowledge is secured by *providence*, God's disposing will toward the world. Ockham asserts in several places that he believes in providence. His conception of God's will, however, gives the content of what he holds by faith a rather unusual twist. He holds that God has both an *antecedent* and a *consequent* disposing will. [OTh IV 671]

By his antecedent will, God wills "the best of all possible worlds": for example, that no human being sin. This will, however, is more like a wish. It can be, and often is, contradicted by what actually happens.

By his consequent will, God wills the world to be exactly as it is. After all, we would not want to say that the world is other than God wills it. If human beings will to sin, then God wills that will.

This twofold conception of God's will more or less empties providence of content. Like a good parent, God has many hopes for us, but he lets us live our own lives.

We put "best of all possible worlds" in scare quotes because Ockham denies that this concept actually makes sense. For every possible world God could come up with, it is always still true that he could come up with yet a better one. [OTh IV 650ff] This just goes to show that it is not God's business to control the world at all, but rather to create a world in which various things can happen, and in which many wills will what they will. In Ockham's view, God is only one of many causes in the world. This implies that the future is *contingent*: it depends on what we do.

Ockham takes it to be fundamental to the Catholic Faith that the future is contingent. Nevertheless, this thesis conflicts with God's foreknowledge. In order to see where the conflict lies, we need to examine the logic of fatalism.

6.4 Fatalism

Ancient Stoic philosophers argued that there is no such thing as contingency in the world. On their view, the logic of future-tense statements implies the doctrine of *fatalism*: that the future is inevitable. The medievals got wind of this reasoning primarily through Aristotle, who gives approximately the following version of the Stoic argument. [*De Interpretatione* 9; in A 96ff.]

If there is a sea battle tomorrow, then it is true right now that there is a sea battle tomorrow. If this is true right now, however, then nothing in the future can change it. After all, nothing that is true right now can ever be changed. If your house is green right now, then nothing that happens in the future can change the fact that your house is green today.

So, if there is a sea battle tomorrow, then it is true now that there is a sea battle tomorrow, and nothing that happens between now and tomorrow can change that fact; so it is inevitable that there will be a sea battle. Likewise, if there is *no* sea battle tomorrow, then it is false right now that there is a sea battle tomorrow. If this is false right now, then nothing in the future can change its falsity. So it is inevitable that there be no sea battle. Either way, the future is inevitable.

In response to this line of reasoning, Aristotle asserts the obvious: that it is not, in fact, necessary that a sea battle will take place tomorrow. Neither is it necessary that a sea battle will not take place tomorrow. The Stoics' unintuitive result follows from the premise that it is now, already, either true or false that there will be a sea battle tomorrow. So Aristotle concludes that the statement, "There will be a sea battle tomorrow," is at the moment neither true nor false.

Ockham, however, thinks this solution odd. Surely every meaningful statement is either true or false. Just because we do not know the future does not mean there is no truth of the matter. Suppose a sea battle happens on March 15, 304 B.C. Then the statement, "A sea battle happens on March 15, 304 B.C.," has been true from all eternity, even though no one knew about it before it happened. So the "no-truth-value" solution will not work. Aristotle is obviously correct, however, in insisting that what will happen tomorrow battle-wise is not inevitable. So, what has gone wrong in the fatalist argument?

It is not immediately clear. It is either true or false that there will be a sea battle tomorrow (say, Tuesday noon.). If it is true, then it is true now (Monday noon) that there will be a sea battle Tuesday noon. Time passes, and it is Tuesday morning. Now (Tuesday morning) it is still the case that it was true on Monday that there will be a sea battle Tuesday noon. So far, so good.

Next, the argument goes on to assume that we cannot change this truth-on-Monday, because it is past, and nobody can change the past. If that statement was true on Monday, and Monday is past, you cannot make it false, no matter what.

But this is where Ockham disagrees. You can prevent the sea battle from occurring, say by ordering your fleet not to engage the enemy.

Suppose you do this. This would prevent the sea battle and make the statement on Monday false.

Yet this is precisely what the original argument supposes to be impossible, on the grounds that you cannot change the past. How can something you do on Tuesday make a statement made on Monday false? If it was true on Monday, then that is a fact about Monday, and nothing that happens on Tuesday can change facts about the past.

Ockham agrees that one cannot influence the past. But, is this not exactly what he supposes happens when your Tuesday decision, as admiral, gives that statement a truth-value on Monday? No.

The reason is that being true is a relational property. Relational properties, as we have seen, have nominal essences. Suppose Sally is the second-smartest person in the class. Now the smartest person in the class leaves town. Suddenly she has changed to being the smartest person in the class, without having gotten any smarter, in fact, without anything actually going on in her at all. Ockham wants to say that propseties such as being the smartest or second-smartest person in the class, are really not in Sally. Each is a relational term personally suppositing inherent qualities (degree of smartness) in particular people in the class, while connoting all the rest of the class too. This is why what might be spoken of as a change in Sally can happen merely by altering these facts about other people.

Likewise, consider an example that involves separate times. Jimmy Carter, born in 1924, became President of the U.S. in 1977. In 1925, Baby Jimmy had the property of being a future president. Nevertheless, what gave him this property happened in 1977: his taking office. How can an event in 1977 give something a property in 1925? Only because it was not a real property inhering in him. It is true that Baby Jimmy was a future president in 1925, but that did not make his later becoming president inevitable. That is because this was not a real property of him in 1925: it was just a nominal essence, something we say was true of him, but not really in him. He had a relational property, depending (in this case wholly) on some things that had yet to happen.

You cannot change the past, of course; that is, you cannot change the facts about inherent properties of real essences in the past. You can make relational changes about the past, however, because these are not wholly about the past.

Return now to the sea battle problem. The so-called fact about the future in question is that on Monday, the sentence "A sea battle happens on Tuesday" is true. If the truth of this sentence on Monday were a real-essence fact about this sentence, then you could not change it later. But, it is not a real fact about this sentence: it is only a relational fact. As Ockham puts it,

> All statements having to do with our fate, whether they are verbally about the present or the past are nevertheless equivalently about the future, since their truth depends on the truth of statements formally about the future. [OPh II 515; A 47]

Granted, statements that convey how things will be are true now and always were true, but they are only contingently true, contingent upon what happens later, which will make them, retroactively, true now. Suppose the statement,

> There will be a sea battle on Tuesday.

was true on Monday. Nevertheless, the fact that this depends on is not a Monday-fact: it is a Tuesday fact. The metalanguage statement,

> The statement, "There will be a sea battle on Tuesday" was true on Monday.

is not about the past because the past includes only real essences, and being true just does not count as one of those. It is about the facts that make it true, and those facts are yet to happen on Tuesday. This is where the fatalist argument goes wrong.

6.5 Foreknowledge

We have seen how Ockham deals with statements about the future in order to avoid the Stoics' fatalist conclusion. He can count them true (or false) despite the openness of the future, because, having future truth conditions, they are made true or false by what happens later. This is to say that they are contingently true or false.

In the case of human beliefs about the future we do not run any risk of fatalism. The reason is that any human belief about the future, even one that turns out true, may have turned out false. Suppose that a very talented meteorologist predicts a tornado and the tornado strikes just as she said it would. Then we may say that the meteorologist knew all along that the tornado was going to strike. Nevertheless, her knowing this did not make the tornado inevitable. The tornado might not have struck. If it had not, we would simply have said that her belief was false—not knowledge about what was going to happen. She did have a belief about what was going to happen; she may have even told people or written it down. The only question was whether or not it would turn out to be true.

The doctrine of omniscience, however, typically counts God's beliefs about the future as necessarily true. This means that the way just indicated to account for human beliefs about the future will not work for God. When God believes something about the future, it must be true; its truth or falsity cannot depend on how things turn out. God's success, after all, should not depend on the way the world happens to work, as human success sometimes does. To say that one of God's beliefs right now might be true or false, depending on how the world works, would impute human imperfection to God.

Given that God necessarily knows every truth about the future, we can run the fatalist argument all over again. The statement "There will be a sea battle tomorrow" is true or false. Because he is omniscient, God has always known that this statement is true (if it is true) or false (if it is false). If God knows on Monday that the sea battle will (or will not) occur on Tuesday, then the sea battle must (or must not) take place on Tuesday.

The difference between logical and theological fatalism is that divine foreknowledge makes the truth of the future-tense statement a real essence, a non-relational part of the past. Bringing about a sea battle on Tuesday will not make it the case retroactively that God's Monday-belief was knowledge. The fact that God knew what will happen tomorrow is a real fact before tomorrow happens. The state of God's mind cannot depend on future contingencies: neither we nor anything else can falsify his beliefs. So God's necessary foreknowledge implies fatalism.

"So much the worse for omniscience!" the contemporary atheist might cry. "All this shows is that there cannot be a God with that attribute." This answer is not open to Ockham, however. He has a real problem. Here is what he says in response:

> For that reason I maintain that it is impossible to express clearly the way in which God knows future contingents. Nevertheless, it must be held that he does, but contingently. This must be held because of the pronouncements of the saints, who say that God does not know things that are going to be in a way different from the way in which he knows things that have already occurred. . . . Although he does know one side of every future-contingent statement, "S or not-S," determinately, nevertheless he knows it contingently in such a way that he can not know it and can never have known it. Therefore, deliberation does make a difference. [OPh II 517-521; A 50-55]

Ockham maintains that God has foreknowledge, it is just not necessary. The fatalist reasons, "If there is a sea-battle tomorrow, God knew this, infallibly, yesterday. If God knew this yesterday, I would make him wrong if I prevented a battle by deciding not to engage the enemy; but I cannot make God wrong, because he is infallible. So why bother to deliberate about what to do? God already knows what will happen, and that is what will happen, regardless of what I decide."

Ockham wants to refute this reasoning. Granted, God already has infallible knowledge about what is going to happen. So, if he already knows that there will be a battle tomorrow, then of course it necessarily follows that there will be a sea battle. It is not necessary, however, that God knows this. He might not-know this; he might know the opposite instead. If the opposite happens, then that is what he will have known. One way or the other, God's past foreknowledge is contingent. Just like past truths about the future, the content of past divine knowledge about the future still depends on what will happen. God's knowledge has only a nominal essence: it is a relational fact about him. This means that the battle facts about tomorrow are still up to you after all; so you had better start deliberating about whether to launch your ships.

It is not clear whether this counts as a solution to the problem or a concession that there is no solution. Ockham admits that it is impossible for any intellect in this life to understand how God's contingent foreknowledge works. He writes,

> It must be maintained that God has evident cognition of all
> future contingents. Yet, I do not know how to describe how he
> does it. Perhaps it can be said that God himself, or the divine
> essence, is a single intuitive cognition . . . a cognition so per-
> fect and so clear that it is also an evident cognition of all
> things past, present, and future. [OTh IV 584-5]

How can there be an intuitive cognition of something that does not yet, and might never, exist? How can God's beliefs be on the one hand contingent for their truth on what will happen, and on the other necessarily infallible? Ockham leaves us to ponder the answer.

Ockham occasionally encounters an intractable problem like this when he discusses the divine attributes. At these places, all he can do is say that ordinary logic does not apply. His final word on the matter is that, if you have to have a kink in the system, it is best to locate it in an area that is supposed to transcend human understanding anyway.

6.6 Ockham Divided

Ockham contends that human beings have no experience of God, that there is no proof of the existence of God, and that some of God's most central attributes make no rational sense. One would suspect that someone in this position would be at least agnostic, if not an unbeliever. Some of Ockham's critics have concluded that he was a secret atheist, and was disingenuous about his commitment to the Church. It would be appropriate for a nominalist to be only a nominal Catholic. We are unable now to ask Ockham what he really thought, and even if we could, he might not have fully revealed it. But careful examination of what Ockham wrote indicates that he was a sincere believer—even if he often failed theology.

Ockham's theological failures should come as no surprise. His first calling was to philosophy, not to theology. It was an accident of history that there was no such thing as a philosophy department in medieval universities. Thinking in terms of the God hypothesis no doubt expanded Ockham's mind, and he takes it as a serious exercise to make his theories fit with the truths of faith. But he did not have a choice about writing about God, and he is ultimately miscast as a theologian.

Ockham wants to have integrity as a philosopher. He becomes stubborn and even bitter whenever religion interferes with his ability to pursue the implications of careful and responsible theorizing. Just as he tries to avoid disturbing matters of religion, he feels that matters of religion should not be allowed to disturb philosophers.

In rejecting supposed demonstrations of the truths of the faith, Ockham's views add up to the position that the medieval efforts to make theology a branch of knowledge, on a par with logic or physics, are utterly hopeless. His overall conclusion is that rational theology is impossible. There is no science of God.

This is what the historians mean when they say that we see in Ockham the disintegration of the medieval worldview. A long line of thinkers from Augustine to Aquinas had slowly built up the hope that the truths of religion could be held equally on the basis of faith or reason, and that neither need be sacrificed for the other. By contrast, Ockham reasons as far as his reasoning will take him, but finds the basic truths of his religion unprovable, and perhaps even incoherent. He insists on acceptance of them anyway, but is careful to bracket them, to isolate them from the rest of philosophy. In so doing, he demonstrates the compartmentalization so characteristic of modern thought.

7

Mind and Freedom

Is Ockham's relentless razoring nothing more than a massive case of spring cleaning? If so, one might wonder what all the fuss is about. After all, theories do not take up any space the way old clothes do. Furthermore, what Ockham trims in one place he often pays for elsewhere. Critics have pointed out, for example, that nominalist supposition theory is much more complicated than its realist counterpart. So why not stick with realism if you want to? What is the harm in preferring an inflated ontology?

There is, in fact, something more at stake in Ockham's program than a tidy workspace. Ockham developed nominalism because he thought it was the only way to save what he took to be the most important thing of all, namely, human freedom.

7.1 Determinism

For Aristotle, forms have explanatory and predictive power. The form something has is responsible for the way it is and what it does. Forms are universals: everything that shares a form will be, and act, the same—in that respect, at least. All humans have inherent in them the same single form of *humanness*, and this determines the same general sort of activity from each of us. There are also sub-classes of humans, defined by more specific universals: *grumpiness, funniness, kindness,* and so on. So each grumpy human shares in the single universal *grumpiness*, and is determined to act in the same grumpy way in certain circumstances. In this way, Aristotelian realism provides a framework for understanding human behavior.

Aristotle himself is notoriously unclear (and perhaps undecided) about his view of human freedom. Nevertheless, Aristotelian realism does seem to imply *determinism*: the position that for any act there were antecedent conditions, whether known or unknown, that were sufficient to guarantee that act. If you have the form of grumpiness, whether you know it or not, you will be grumpy when confronted with certain circumstances. The grumpiness in you necessarily causes grumpy behavior.

Ockham was unwaveringly convinced that determinism is false. He thinks that things like grumpiness, kindness, and humor are a matter of free choice.

We have already seen how nominalism helps Ockham resist determinism. No two individual things (or people) share a single form. We classify things on the basis of resemblance of their forms, and this classification will allow prediction on the basis of the Principle of Induction: "Every individual of the same kind has an effect of the same kind." It is always an open question, however, whether two individuals are of the same kind. After a number of observations of close similarities, we are entitled to predict that they are, and that they will continue to manifest the same effects. Nevertheless, generalizations and predictions based on observation are, for Ockham, inductive, empirical, contingent, and fallible.

Moreover, necessity is a matter of how we define things. Everything of a certain kind must act according to the nature of that kind. But it does not follow that any particular thing must necessarily act any particular way. All that follows is that *if* that particular thing is a member of a kind, *then* it will act the way that kind of thing acts (by definition).

Nevertheless, Ockham does believe that science should and can produce reliable explanations and predictions. His Principle of Induction does presuppose a causal regularity in the world. Fish swim, birds fly. The pattern is contingent, but stable enough to confirm our scientific habits of mind, by which we deduce characteristic behaviors.

According to Ockham, all natural objects have intrinsic forms, which he sees as powers, or dispositions. Sometimes these dispositions will determine change only in response to external circumstances, as when a pumpkin is disposed to turn orange when it gets sufficient sunlight. Sometimes these dispositions determine change from the inside without an external push, as when a battery-operated clock will tick off the seconds; this is not a response to external stimuli but is merely a consequence of the internal setup of the clock. In both sorts of cases, however, if we trace back the causal chains involved, the object's behavior is externally determined: the clock's by its internal nature, which is itself determined by the way it was manufactured; the pumpkin's by sunlight plus its genetics.

It appears that humans, being natural objects themselves, are also determined in these ways. Some human activities are determined by external pushes. Roger has the disposition to sunburn, so spending time outdoors will cause his skin to turn red. An external force, given the particular nature of his skin, causes this effect in him. Some human activities are determined by internal facts that are themselves determined. As he ages, Roger's hair falls out. This is the result of a genetic predisposition built into him at conception. Granted, this varies in humans, and there is no guarantee that it will happen to Roger, but if it does, it will have been caused by his nature.

If everything human beings do is like this, then we are no freer than every other natural thing in the nominalist's universe. Our internally-caused behavior comes from our nature. Our externally-caused behavior comes from environmental stimuli plus our nature. And if our natures themselves come from genetics and upbringing, then the way we behave is traceable back to causal factors outside us.

7.2 The Human Difference

Ockham is convinced that external causes cannot be the source of all human behavior. If they were, we would not be any more responsible for what we do than pumpkins are for what they do. If the causal chain determining our actions starts outside us, then we are passive victims of external efficient causes. Ockham writes,

> Lower life forms do not have free choice because they do not act but rather are acted upon. . . . That is, their acts are not in their power and they do not have ownership of them. And this gets right to the point. Those who have free will have ownership and power over their acts. [OTh I 502]

For us to be responsible for how we act, we must be the ultimate authors of our own actions: we must be unmoved movers.

Aristotle famously claimed that there is only one unmoved mover, namely God. Ockham nevertheless finds a way to interpret The Philosopher to his own purpose. He writes,

> It should be noted here first that the Philosopher does not intend simply to deny that something can be moved by itself, at least by extending "move" to sudden change. For our will

62

changes itself due to this: that within itself it causes a volition. For since no exterior act is praiseworthy or blameworthy unless because it is in our power, according to the Philosopher in Book III of the *Ethics*, it is fitting also that no act of loving or of hating is praiseworthy or blameworthy unless because it is in our power. It is manifest, however, that the act of loving another sometimes is praiseworthy and sometimes is blameworthy. Therefore, such an act is in our power. If it were caused by something else naturally and sufficiently, however, it would not be in our power. It remains therefore that such an act is in some way effectively from the will. And in this way the will in itself causes such acts and thus moves itself. [OPh V 598]

People are free, according to Ockham, insofar as their actions are *wholly* internally caused. It is not sufficient to have an internal cause of the sort the clock manifests when it ticks off the seconds. The ticking is caused by the clock's internal nature, but this internal nature is caused by the way the clock was manufactured. An action for which a human being is responsible must be entirely internally generated. The chain of causes must stop within the person.

Ockham is an unambiguous *metaphysical libertarian*: he thinks that determinism is false because it is incompatible with free choice. Here is a passage in which Ockham explicitly states his commitment to libertarianism, and explains how he supposes it to work:

The will is freely able to will something and not to will it. By this I mean that it is able to destroy the willing that it has and produce anew a contrary effect, or it is equally able in itself to continue that same effect and not produce a new one. It is able to do all of this without any prior change in the intellect, or in the will, or in something outside them. The idea is that the will is equal for producing and not producing because, with no difference in antecedent conditions, it is able to produce and not to produce. It is poised equally over contrary effects in such a way, in fact, that it is able to cause love or hatred of something. . . . To deny every agent this equal or contrary power is to destroy every praise and blame, every council and deliberation, every freedom of the will. Indeed, without it, the will would not make a human being free any more than appetite does an ass. [OPh IV 319-321]

7.3 Buridan's Ass

Ockham maintains that free choice is one of the central differences between human beings and lower life forms. During the fourteenth century, there was widespread debate on this issue. Throughout the course of the debate, a thought experiment known as "Buridan's Ass" came into currency. It is named after Jean Buridan (c. 1295 - 1356), a younger contemporary of Ockham's, and it goes like this.

Imagine a very hungry donkey poised between two equally attractive piles of hay. The donkey has one desire: to go to the nearest pile of hay. But the piles are equally distant. So despite the wealth of hay nearby, the donkey will starve to death.

Human beings do not get themselves stuck in such fixes. Imagine, for example, that you are in the supermarket to buy a can of your favorite brand of tomato soup. There are dozens of cans of that brand of soup arrayed before you, absolutely similar ones as far as you can tell. Yet, you do pick one.

What the libertarian wants to conclude from this thought experiment is that the deterministic model of choice, in which choice is caused by antecedent conditions, must (in the case of humans) be incorrect. For if it were correct, then equally powerful but opposed conditions would result in paralysis. But, in reality, it almost never does.

Libertarians argue that the reason why humans are not paralyzed by tie-making conditions is that we have free will, while donkeys do not. Freedom enables human beings to break ties.

It might be objected, however, that very few of our actions involve breaking ties. How often, after all, do we get into situations in which alternatives are so precisely balanced as to produce no inclination in us to go one way or the other?

The libertarian would reply: very often. Imagine yourself in a choice situation. Say, for example, that you need a new car, and are considering what sort to buy. You could buy an expensive, zippy sports car, or an economical, reliable sedan. Suppose that you are a cautious, practical sort of person. Then, it would seem that the sedan would be the alternative that you would automatically be inclined towards. Or, if you are the irresponsible, fun-loving, live-for-the-moment sort, then the sports car would impose itself on you as the more attractive alternative. Either way, it seems that things are hardly balanced.

But when you imagine yourself in this situation, you realize that you are in a position to decide what sort of person you want to be. Suppose that, in the past, you have always been the responsible sort. It is now up to you to decide whether you want to continue with this personality or not. You have the power to go either way. You can make yourself into either sort of person. If you were innately, necessarily, essentially a responsible person, then things would clearly be tilted strongly for the sedan. But the fact that you can now make yourself into either sort of person means that things are in balance, and you are free.

Now we can see why Ockham's nominalism provides such a crucial foundation for his account of human freedom. In the example we are considering, the determinist imagines that you have one personality or the other—that you have some form—and that this power or disposition to act will result in a characteristic action in the circumstance under consideration. If you have the form *responsibleness,* you will buy the sedan. If you have the form *fun-lovingness,* you will buy the sports car. For the realist, the choice is determined. On Ockham's view, in contrast, to say that an individual has a form is to say only that it has resembled certain other things. You have the form *responsibleness* if you happen to have resembled other sedan-buyers. But it is contingent matter which form you have, and therefore, whom you resemble from now on.

How, then, does one form or the other arise in you now that it is time to buy a car? The answer is: you create it. This is how you are an unmoved mover, and why you are free. Your freedom here is a matter generating an intention, and this is what makes you different from lower life forms. Ockham writes,

> Natural agents proceed anew from rest into action at the moment when an impediment is removed. For instance, wood starts burning because a fire is now close to it and previously was not. In contrast, a free agent proceeds anew into action because he begins to intend an end. [OTh IX 300; Q 249]

7.4 Compatibilism

What we have just seen illustrates vividly the difference between Ockham's position and *compatibilism,* the version of determinism that most philosophers nowadays hold. Compatibilists typically count an action as free just insofar as it is the result of the agent's decision, and thus the consequence of his own values, as opposed to the result of external force. Suppose that it has been built into you, either through your genes or through your upbringing, to be responsible. Then you will necessarily choose the sedan. Compatibilists still count this choice as "free," however, because no one forced you from the outside (say, by literally pushing you).

Whereas most contemporary compatibilists see environment, genes and upbringing as the causal factors of human behavior, theological compatibilists see God as the cause. Despite this, they count some actions as "free" because the causal chain includes human decision. For example, God could physically compel you to go to church. This would not be a free act because it would be externally forced upon you. God could also cause you to decide to go to church, however. This would be a free act, according to theological compatibilists.

But not according to Ockham. If God caused it, then you did not cause it, and you are not responsible. [OTh VI 388-389] In order for it to be your act, you must be able to do otherwise. Ockham's objections to contemporary compatibilism would be similar. He would insist that what compatibilists count as "free" actions—those whose causal chain includes the agent's decision—are not really free if that decision was caused by the circumstances plus the agent's character, and if the agent's character were itself caused by genes and upbringing. Real free action is action whose causal chain has its beginning inside agents, who are thus unmoved movers. When agents create evaluations, they thereby create their own nature.

Ockham is virtually alone among medieval philosophers in rejecting compatibilism. Some openly embrace determinism, others try to avoid it and fail, either because they have no grasp of nominalism or because they feel pressure from the Church. Ockham, in contrast, is happy to admit that a good deal of the way we are and what we do comes from God and from inborn or acquired inclinations; but not our freely-willed actions. For those, we are the origins.

This is really saying something, because Ockham has a very strong view of God's power. But he insists that not even God can cause your intention in such a way that it is still *your* intention. If you did not make it *ex nihilo* then it simply is not yours.

What it comes down to is that Ockham's notion of origination cannot be understood as anything less than a kind of creation. He writes,

> This is when you produce some effect in such a way that, with no variation in you or in anything else, you have just as much power not to produce it as you do to produce it. Neither act is determined by your nature. [OTh I 502]

Ockham was reluctant to call human beings "creators," since we do not make *things* like God does, out of nothing. [OTh IX 150-6; Q 126-32] Nevertheless, he calls us "producers" because we do make *acts* out of nothing just as God does.

66

7.5 The Soul

Ockham has claimed that the free choice of human beings originates in their wills. Traditionally, the will is considered a proper part of the soul (or mind). Ockham was eager to make sure he had a coherent account of it.

Aristotle's remarks about the soul are cryptic and inconclusive. Every natural object consists of matter and form. So, if we think of the body as the matter, then we can think of the soul as the form. During the Middle Ages, however, there was considerable pressure to come up with an account of the soul that would make sense of the Christian doctrine that human beings survive the death of their bodies. It was a bit of a trick to make an immanent form into the kind of thing that can exist independently of its matter in that way.

Aquinas, whose interpretations of Aristotle were, of course, enormously influential, asserts that a single and unified form of *humanness* is shared by all human beings. A person comes to be when this universal is individuated by matter. Then, when the matter dies away, the individuated form can live on in heaven, should it be so lucky.

Unfortunately, Aquinas's attempt to combine Aristotle with Christianity results in a picture of the human person that he did not intend. It suggests that the body is a passive object, a container for the soul that moves it around and eventually leaves it. Aquinas himself tried to avoid this picture because it presents the soul's actions as efficient cause of bodily movements, and thus goes against the Aristotelian idea that the form of a substance is a formal cause that brings about change from the inside. Nevertheless, Aquinas's claim that the soul is the single animating principle of the body tended to reinforce this picture of mover and thing moved.

We see, then, in Aquinas, the roots of what has come to be known as *dualism*, the idea that a human being is made of two very different kinds of things: the body is an inert hunk of material, and the soul is its immaterial driver. This is the idea that Descartes would become famous for developing and defending.

7.6 Human Plurality

Ockham preferred to read Aristotle as rejecting the view that the soul was a unified principle of motion, pushing the body it inhabited. In his view, forms are individual powers. A human being consists in the collaboration of three substantial forms:

1. The corporeal power, by which we extend through space, move downward by gravity, and otherwise act like physical objects;

2. The sentient power, by which we sense our environment and feel aversion and attraction, as animals do;

3. The intellective power, by which we reason and will.

A rock cannot do much more than resist penetration and roll downhill; it is a corporeal power. An armadillo can do these things and, in addition, can sense its environment; it is a corporeal-sentient power. A human can do all this, plus reason and will; it is a corporeal-sentient-intellective power.

Because the intellective power is one held by human beings alone (among earthly objects), it is important. It includes volition, which is the power to exercise preferences, and, more importantly in this case, to *create* values and desires. Lower life forms and inanimate objects are determined because they do not have this power. It is this power, Ockham thinks, that demarcates genuine acts of will from mere behavior.

In Ockham's view, then, a human being is an individual quantity with three substantive forms. Fred is not an inert hunk of matter with a mind somehow "inserted" into it. Body is not a *thing* at all but rather a power, just as is mind. Fred is more like a field in which several sorts of powers and their associated acts can happen at the same time. Just as a light bulb can both light and heat, Fred can both move and think.

Ockham had an argument to show that the corporeal, sentient, and intellective powers of human existence are independent forms rather than a single individuated universal form. There cannot be contradictory tendencies within a single form, yet contradictory tendencies exist in a human being. Ockham writes,

> It is manifest that an act of desiring and an act of spurning exist simultaneously in a human being, since a human being spurns by his intellective appetite the very same thing that he desires by his sentient appetite. [OTh IX 157; Q 132-133]

Ockham has in mind a familiar experience like wanting very badly a second slice of banana cream pie while at the same time thinking that a second slice is a very bad idea. Since one and the same power cannot do contradictory things at the same time, the intellective and sensory forms must be distinct powers.

As for the corporeal form, we know of its independent existence from the fact that when something dies, its body lingers for a while. Ockham writes,

68

> When a human being or an animal dies, numerically the same
> accidents remain as were there previously; therefore, they
> have numerically the same subject. . . . Therefore, some form
> that was there previously remains, and it is not the sentient
> one, so it is the corporeal one. [OTh IX 162; Q 137]

Does that recently deceased armadillo exist or not? It seems, yes, since
the very same body is sitting right over there, but, it seems, no, since it
does not do what it used to do. Ockham's solution: the corporeal form
still exists and the sentient form does not. It still exists as a corporeal
power, but not as a sentient one.

In Ockham's view, then, bodies and minds are both powers, the
former of extending through space, weighing, and so on, and the latter
of reasoning and willing. Ockham deliberately speaks of the corporeal
form as the "corporeal soul." And it is the corporeal-sentient-
intellective soul as a whole that inheres in and animates the individual
quantity that is a human being. Ockham writes, "A soul that is a corporeal form suffices to move the body by local motion; therefore, it is
superfluous to posit another mover." [OTh IX 65; Q 57] What he
means is that physical motion is a power of certain natural physical
objects, and is fully explainable by the corporeal form of the physical
object. Human bodily motion, then, is explainable in the same way: by
the normal sorts of physical pushes and pulls. In the case of organisms,
this is organic motion. We are also capable of "movements" of the intellect, however, when we come to desire or believe something. These
mental movements are explained by the intellective power. Both sorts
of movements are done by the same thing, the human being, in which
both powers lie.

It is also possible to conceive of something with an intellective but
no corporeal power. Angels, according to the medieval tradition, are
like this. Since their minds do not come with bodies, they are forced to
borrow unused bodies when they deliver messages on earth. Ockham
understands angels' motion in what amounts to the dualists' picture: the
mind occupies an extrinsic body, and commands motion in it, piloting
it around. [OTh IX 371-5; Q 307-10] Ockham calls this "inorganic motion" (and if you look at medieval pictures of angels flying stiffly
through the air you will see for yourself just how inorganic it is). Ockham is interested in inorganic motion in so far as it is needed to save
certain articles of faith, but it does not come to play in his physics or in
his picture of human beings at all.

On Ockham's view, then, nominalism provides the foundation for
a coherent account of human action. By denying that natural objects

have universal essences, Ockham preserves contingency in their behavior. But human beings are an especially powerful sort of natural object. Due to the intellective power of reason and will, we make choices. The contingency we face is the contingency of conscious self-determination. Ockham's view resonates well with that of the twentieth-century libertarian Jean-Paul Sartre (1905-1980). We are what we make ourselves to be.

8
Ethics

Ockham's ethics is an interesting mixture of the conservative and the radical. His starting point is his commitment to Catholicism. Ockham was a priest, after all, and had no desire to contradict the Church or the conventional wisdom of the day. Nevertheless, Ockham was also deeply committed to nominalism. The nominalist principles he laid down in his logic, epistemology, and metaphysics led him to surprising conclusions in ethics.

8.1 Divine Command

As we saw in chapter six, Ockham argues that there is no science of theology in so far as this involves speculation about God. This is because we do not experience God directly and hence have no evident knowledge of him. But we do have direct experience and evident knowledge of value. Ockham argues, therefore, that in so far as theology concerns itself with value theory, or ethics, it is a science. He writes,

> Moral learning is a demonstrative science. . . . I claim further
> that this science is more certain than many others because all
> of us are able to have more experience of our own acts than of
> other things. The obvious implication is that this science is
> very subtle, useful, and evident. [OTh IX 178; Q 149-50]

Ethics, unlike religion, is not just a matter of faith.

Ockham's scientific approach to ethics makes him an objectivist. As such, he would have been strongly opposed to some views popular nowadays: that right and wrong are only in the eye of the beholder or are only social constructs; that ethical statements are never either true or false, but are merely expressions of feelings. He took it as an obvious fact that some things really are right and some things really are wrong, whatever anyone's opinion about the matter happens to be.

But this raises the age-old question that every ethical objectivist is forced to answer: What makes a right act right? Ockham finds his answer in *divine command theory*. He holds that a right act is an act that is loved and commanded by God.

Divine command theory is probably the least popular approach to ethics in the entire history of philosophy. Even in the Middle Ages, when Christianity was at its zenith, many philosopher-theologians sought alternatives. The reason is that there are some fairly obvious objections to it. We pause to mention the most important of them here.

8.2 Objections

OBJECTION 1:

Plato's *Euthyphro* contains what many philosophers consider the decisive refutation of divine command theory. In this dialogue, Euthyphro claims that a certain action is good because it is loved by the gods. Socrates, however, asks Euthyphro why the gods love that action. In so doing, he reveals the circularity in Euthyphro's thinking: Euthyphro admits that the gods love the act because it is good.

Plato is, in effect, arguing that it cannot be that God's loving something is what makes it right, because if it were not already right, God would not love it. It appears that divine command theory has things backwards. It is not that something is right because God commands it. It is that God commands something because it is right.

Is this refutation really decisive? Ockham did not know of the Euthyphro dialogue. Yet, if he had, he might have had a response: How do things get their rightness if not from God? This is a good question, which opponents of divine command theory have trouble answering. More than two thousand years of philosophy have not yielded a widely convincing answer. Ockham reasons that if there is going to be a mystery involved, we may as well keep it contained in religious quarters.

OBJECTION 2:

According to divine command theorists, goodness just is whatever God loves. So to praise the goodness of that love would be like exclaiming over the fact that the standard meter-stick happens to be exactly one meter long. God's will could not be measured against the standard for morality if God's will were the standard for morality. This seems counter-intuitive to most theists.

Ockham might admit that divine command theory makes the Christian tenet that God is perfectly good into a tautology. He would be quick to point out, however, that divine command theory does not imply that God is less than perfectly good. In fact, it is impossible for God to be less than perfectly good. This seems a fitting property for the divinity.

OBJECTION 3:

Nevertheless, we can generate a further challenge from this answer. If it is impossible for God to be less than perfectly good, then anything he commanded would necessarily be good. What if he commanded us to torture innocent children? Surely torturing innocent children is wrong!

Ockham would agree that torturing innocent children is wrong. He would insist, however, that this is because God *in fact* commands us not to do it. To claim that God *cannot* command us to torture innocent children would be to deny God's omnipotence. God can do anything that is logically possible and it is not logically impossible for God to command things we consider evil. Ockham writes,

> I reply that hatred, theft, adultery, and the like, may involve
> evil according to the common law, in so far as they are done
> by someone who is obligated by a divine command to perform
> the opposite act. As far as everything absolute in these actions
> is concerned, however, God can perform them without in-
> volving any evil. And they can even be performed meritori-
> ously by someone on earth if they should fall under a divine
> command, just as now the opposite of these, in fact, fall under
> a divine command. [OTh V 352]

Ockham accepts the full force of this challenge to divine command theory, insisting that the difference between what God could do and what he actually does do should be sufficient to placate our intuitions.

It is evident from these objections that Ockham faced some serious controversy in adopting divine command theory. Why did he do it? Does divine command theory offer a significant advantage that makes it worth the trouble?

8.3 The Contingency of the Rules

As always, when Ockham talks about what God can or cannot do, he is referring to the difference between the possible and the impossible. So when he says that God might have commanded the torture of innocent children but did not, he is stressing the contingency of the moral judgement that such torture is wrong.

In the Middle Ages, as now, most people thought of morality as a matter of universal and eternal rules. Even those who think of God as the ultimate source of these rules typically see them as necessary and applying without exception. Ockham does not. By conceiving God's command as the source of ethics, Ockham renders the rules contingent. This makes for a revolutionary morality in three ways.

First, it suggests that conventional and widespread judgements about right and wrong might be entirely incorrect. Even when society is unanimous about some matter of morality, if this conflicts with God's will, then society is wrong. Theories basing the legitimacy of a moral code on social agreement cannot come to this conclusion; a theory based on divine command, in contrast, can oppose even the most powerful social forces. This happened in the case of Martin Luther (1483-1546), who, incidentally, studied Ockham and admired him very much.

But secondly: Ockham's position allows that God can change his mind. It is logically possible for God to command one thing one day and another thing the next. Hence, we can tailor our judgements to the circumstances as we experience them. What had been forbidden for a very long time may now be permissible. In this way, Ockham's theory promotes change and growth in our conception of right and wrong.

And thirdly, Ockham's theory implies that God can make individual exceptions and allowances. God may deem one act of killing wrong and another one right, or one and the same act of killing wrong for one person but right for another. The point is that ethical judgements are about particular acts, not general kinds of acts. Every act must be considered unique.

The contingency in Ockham's ethical theory can be understood as a consequence of his nominalism. When God wills that a particular act is good, we might want to generalize over this, and conclude that other acts *of the same kind* are also good. On Ockham's view, however, all "sameness" must be understood in terms of similarity and it becomes an open question which acts are sufficiently similar to the first one. Ockham's ethics, then, differs from many other views in that it is an *act theory*, as opposed to a *rule theory*. Ockham encourages serious consideration of the morality of each act individually, as opposed to a mechanical application of a general ethical principle to individual cases.

8.4 The Open Question

The contingency of ethical judgement implies that any ethical theory that attempts to produce a single criterion of right action must be incorrect. Ockham's theory does not do this, despite counting right action as what God wills, because God does not will in accordance with any overriding principle. Ockham writes,

> Mortal sin does not have a real-essence definition, but only a nominal-essence definition. For there is no one real thing whether positive or privative or negative that it signifies. Rather, it signifies many things that have no unity, either through themselves or through association. [OTh VII 195]

This means that there is no intrinsic nature that makes something, in itself, good or evil. It is only by relation to God's will that something acquires a moral property. "Sin" and other ethical words will thus have only a nominal definition, signifying deliberately willing against God's will.

A long-standing ethical tradition counts certain natural characteristics as necessarily making an action right. A natural characteristic is, in this context, an empirically observable characteristic that a thing possesses of its own accord, independently of human judgement. A theory rooted in this tradition is called *ethical naturalism*.

A clear example of ethical naturalism is provided by Aristotle, who identifies moral rightness with the proper functioning of human beings. Another example is utilitarianism, which, in various versions, identifies moral rightness with promoting pleasure.

G. E. Moore (1873-1958) was an important twentieth-century critic of naturalism, and his arguments will make a useful comparison to Ockham's. Moore accused naturalists of committing the "naturalistic fallacy": the identification of the right-making property with some other property, a natural one. This identification, he argued, cannot be a matter of definition. Suppose it is proposed that "right action" is defined as action that promotes pleasure. Then it would be empty to ask, "Is this act of promoting pleasure really the right action?" The answer would be "Obviously yes, by definition." Compare the emptiness of the question: "Is Fred's brother male?" But the ethical question is always a good question, not an empty, senseless one. It is an "open question" whose answer is not obvious. So the natural property could not be associated with rightness merely by definition. Nor was Moore sympathetic with any Aristotelian attempt to make the identification of rightness with any natural characteristic a matter of metaphysical necessity.

He had to conclude that rightness could not be identified with any natural property in any way.

Likewise, on Ockham's view, even if a certain category of things (for example, acts of kindness) turned out always to be right, this would not be a matter of necessity. The only thing that could confer necessity on this sort of generalization, for Ockham, would be if it were true as a matter of definition. Suppose that "murder" is defined as an act of wrongful killing. Then, of course, it would be true by definition, and thus analytically necessary, that any instance of murder is wrong. That would not, however, imply that this particular killing is wrong, because a particular killing is not necessarily a murder. To find out that it is a murder, we would first have to find out if it is wrong. For Ockham, just as for Moore, it is an open question whether an act with any natural characteristic is right or wrong.

If the rightness of an action is not a natural property, then what sort of property is it? Moore, not very helpfully, tells us that it is a non-natural property and leaves it at that. Ockham, on the other hand, can tell us exactly why rightness is not natural, and what sort of property it is: it is a supernatural property. As a fourteenth-century thinker, Ockham has access to a well-established conceptual language, full of rich associations, for referring to properties other than the mundane, natural ones; the twentieth-century decline of religion has made this language mostly unavailable. Where Moore shrugs, Ockham has something to say.

8.5 The Virtuous Person

If Ockham's ethics were based entirely on unnatural properties it would be very difficult for him to maintain his scientific approach. How does one detect an unnatural property? (Moore, unhelpfully again, refers to "intuition.") But a substantial portion of Ockham's ethics is naturalistic. For although the rightness and wrongness of actions is an unnatural property, the goodness and badness of persons is not.

The virtuous, according to Ockham, are not those who merely perform actions that are commanded by God, but rather, those who perform actions that are commanded by God precisely *because* they are commanded by God. Suppose God wills that you go to church, and you go to church, but not because God wills it, rather, because you want people to think you are holy. This is actually one of Ockham's favorite examples of covert vice. [E.g., OTh VIII 329; W 71] Even though you are doing the thing with the right supernatural property, you are not doing it because it has that property, and hence you are not virtuous.

76

Conversely, suppose you go to church tirelessly all your life because you think God wants you to, but, as it happens, he does not. This is a kind of virtue, tragic perhaps, but virtue nonetheless. In Ockham's system, virtue concerns the intentions behind the action. As a moral agent, you are evaluated according to how faithfully you are following your conscience.

The evaluation of someone who does wrong believing it is right was a matter of considerable debate in Ockham's day. Ockham argues:

> A created will that follows an invincibly erroneous conscience is a right will; for the divine will wills that it should follow conscience when conscience is blameless. If it acts against that conscience, then it sins because it is obliged not to act against conscience. [OTh VII 436]

When he says "invincibly erroneous conscience" he has in mind people who really thought they were obeying God's will and had no way of knowing they were not. This makes good sense of the value we intuitively place on "meaning well."

8.6 Ethical Rationalism and Empiricism

The rationalism/empiricism distinction in epistemology may be used to provide a rough distinction between kinds of ethical theory: those that hold that we determine right and wrong through sense-observation, and those that hold that it is determined a-priori. There is a close connection between ethical empiricism and ethical naturalism, the position that the ethical properties are ordinary natural ones; for those are the properties which our available to our senses.

Positioning Ockham in this controversy is not a simple matter. In some ways, he is quite explicitly anti-empiricist. He identifies the rightness of an action with that action's being willed by God, and he is very clear in insisting that ordinary folk like us have no direct way to find out what God wills. Ockham is willing to allow the possibility that God communicated with the prophets, but not with the rest of us. So how do we find out that an action is right?

Ockham uses the phrase "right reason" in discussing the process whereby one can reliably arrive at ethical truth. This makes him sound like a rationalist, because "right reason" is the phrase rationalists often use to refer to the wholly a-priori methods human beings use to discover ethical truth.

On the other hand, the rest of Ockham's epistemology makes it unlikely that he would consider himself an ethical rationalist. He restricts the class of truths discoverable by reason alone to those that are implied by the concepts involved; that is, he claims that the only a-priori truths are analytic; but if ethical truths depend on God's contingent will, they cannot be analytic.

So how do we discover ethical facts? There are two kinds of ethical facts: facts about the action and facts about the person performing the action. The latter concern virtue, which is a natural characteristic, and hence not too difficult to observe. You can tell by looking into peoples' eyes whether they are sincerely intending to do the right thing for the right reason. But what about the former? Surely we are sometimes in a position to say, "You clearly meant well, but you did the wrong thing." Setting aside the value of the person, how do we judge the value of the act?

Ockham does not offer any simple recipes. We are supposed to be able to tell whether or not an act is ethical by inspecting it. When we inspect it, however, we will not find an intrinsic, natural property that makes it ethical. Rather, we will find a relational property. Act x is ethical if and only if it is something God loves and commands. Goodness is a nominal essence. Furthermore, it is not even a natural nominal essence, like being-the-tallest-girl-in-the-class. The relation at stake is a relation to a supernatural being.

This is deeply puzzling. Ordinarily, detecting relational properties requires inspection of all the relata involved. But in ethical cases, one relatum, God, is inaccessible. How does this ethical empiricism work? Ockham does not tell us.

Perhaps we can think of the ethical property in an act more along the lines of a quality than a relation. A group of individuals can be similar with respect to *blueness*, even though we have never experienced *blueness* itself. This is because each individual contains its own particular blue color. Perhaps godliness is a really inherent quality like color. Then a group of actions can be similar with respect to godliness, despite God's inaccessibility. Of course, Ockham will not want to push this analogy too far since, according to his system, blueness is a universal that exists only in the mind, whereas God is supposed to exist outside the mind.

8.7 Rationalism (2)

Insofar as Socrates (470-399 B.C.) was a mouthpiece for Plato's moral epistemology, he was an ethical rationalist as characterized above. But Socrates was also an ethical rationalist in a second sense. This second position is often summed up by the slogan: virtue is knowledge and evil is ignorance.

This type of ethical rationalism makes the following assessment. In any choice situation involving a good and an evil alternative, our reasoning powers, when they are working right, will show us that the good alternative is good and the evil one evil. When they do this, they automatically provide us with a conclusive rationale for doing the good action. Somebody who did not have a conclusive rationale for doing the good action must not actually realize that it is a good action.

Various philosophers throughout history have proposed softer versions of this view, Aristotle included. The best way to explain the controversy about this kind of ethical rationalism is to contrast the positions of Ockham and Aquinas. Aquinas considered himself to be following Aristotle, and is perhaps the most famous ethical rationalist of the medieval period.

Aquinas thought that it was too simplistic to reduce evil to ignorance alone. Sometimes a person knows perfectly well that it would be wrong to do something, but he goes ahead and does it anyway. This is the phenomenon Aristotle called "*akrasia*," often translated as "weakness of will," though, as we shall see, that does not exactly describe Aquinas's account of knowingly doing wrong. Aquinas gives an example:

> Suppose someone is debating in his mind whether or not to have sex with this woman. He may judge, still speculating in the realm of principles, that this would be evil. However, when he comes to apply this judgement to the act, many circumstances relevant to the act present themselves from all sides, for instance, the pleasure of the sex. This desire may constrain his reason so that its dictates do not issue into choice. [T 329]

In Aquinas's view, when people know the better and choose the worse, they are allowing desire to cloud reason. Hence, although evil is sometimes a result of ignorance, it is also sometimes a result of temporary confusion caused by desire. Despite this corrective to Socrates, Aquinas agrees with him that people never purposely do what they know to be evil. In cases where desire competes with and triumphs over reason, it does so precisely because it makes something *appear* good.

8.8 Voluntarism

It was Augustine (354-430) who first articulated opposition to this form of rationalism. He launched the opposing medieval tradition of *voluntarism,* which maintains that the will can resist reason, and can deliberately choose evil apart from any ignorance or irrational desire.

According to voluntarists, it is just wishful thinking to suppose that human beings never choose what they deem bad. It would certainly be nice if they did not, but can we really make sense of the evil in the world by attributing it to stupidity or confusion?

Ockham agrees with Augustine that we cannot. In Ockham's estimation, the rationalist view is a naive armchair account of what is actually going on out there. Ockham writes:

> I say that the will is able to will a bad thing that is neither really nor apparently good, and is able to will against a good thing that is neither really nor apparently bad. [OTh VIII 443]

Ockham argues that those who claim that it is automatic (or even necessary) that one will whatever one takes to be good are really taking this as a definitional truth, and understanding the word "good" in a nonstandard way. He writes,

> In another way, "good" just means the same as whatever is willed, or is understood for all that which is willable. . . . The authorities and the doctors who say that the will is not able to will something unless it is really or apparently good can be glossed thus. [OTh VIII 442-6]

For Ockham, it is an inherent part of human freedom to be able to accept or reject goodness at any time. This is because the will (not to be confused with a temporary, irrational desire) is stronger than reason. What is his proof? He writes,

> The thesis in question cannot be proved by any argument, since every argument meant to prove it will assume something that is just as unknown as, or more unknown than, the conclusion. Nonetheless, the thesis can be known evidently through experience, since a human being experiences that, no matter how much reason dictates a given thing, the will is still able to will that thing, or not to will it, or to will against it. [OTh IX 88; Q 132]

It is an entirely empirical matter. Anyone who introspects knows it.

Ockham's voluntarism connects with his metaphysical libertarianism. As we saw in the last chapter, Ockham claimed that the will is free only when it is not determined by any rationale, no matter how strong. If knowledge that some act is good provides a rationale for doing it, this does not determine the will to choose it. We still have the act of free choice over and above whatever rationale there is.

So Ockham's picture is this: we can know the facts of moral action and yet not act morally. What is necessary in addition is that we make these objective goods *our* goods by loving them. We perform what is an act of will, not merely of understanding.

8.9 Love

What ultimately attracted Ockham to divine command theory is that it makes love its highest priority over and above reasons and rules. A strong element in the Christian tradition that Ockham embraces is the idea that morality is a matter of relations between persons. God's will is loving, and his central command is that we love one another.

Ockham uses the concept of true friendship (*amor amicitiae*) to characterize morality. True friendship is the love by which you appreciate people as ends in themselves rather than using them merely as the means to an end. Ockham spends a great deal of energy criticizing theories that fail to keep relationships between persons from becoming instrumental. [E.g., OTh 371, ff.] In this (as in his emphasis on motive, discussed in section 8.5 above), he very much anticipates Immanuel Kant (1724-1804).

The main purpose of divine command theory is to set up a perfect paradigm for human beings to follow. Ockham often says that to obey God's commands is simply to love as God loves. How does God love? Without ulterior motive. God does not need us for anything. He is sufficient unto himself. He benefits us completely gratuitously. His love is true love because it is absolutely selflessly given.

8.10 Going to Hell

Ockham talks as though he firmly believes in heaven and hell. [E.g., Quod 1.19, where Ockham struggles to explain how a spirit feels the heat of the fire in Purgatory.] This would seem to undermine his claim that moral action is not instrumentally motivated. If your motive for acting morally toward others is to go to heaven and avoid hell, then it seems you are treating people as means to your end after all.

The doctrine of heaven and hell does not play that role in Ockham's system, however. There are two reasons. First of all, the contingency of God's will leaves human beings without any reassurances. Ockham insists that God does not have to reward good behavior or punish evil behavior. There is no point in being good for personal benefit, in his view, because God just might welcome all the bad guys into heaven and throw the good guys into hell. [E.g., Quod 6.4] Second, even supposing you think that unlikely to happen, the promise of reward and threat of punishment need not be your motives for action. If they were, you were not good after all, according to Ockham.

8.11 Ockham for Atheists

Critics of divine command theory often complain that it leaves atheists out of the loop, without a chance of being moral. Ockham, however, is especially concerned to include non-believers in his theory. He maintains that non-believers can act in accordance with right reason, and that they are virtuous in so far as they perform those acts for the sake of right reason. [OTh VIII 355; W 111] Right reason is actually identical to God's will. Those who realize this achieve the "highest level" of virtue. Nevertheless, those who do not can lead an exactly parallel existence. Ockham insists that it cannot be proven that faith in a supernatural being is required for the good life. [OTh VI 279]

Ockham's basic point seems to be that everyone, theist and atheist alike, has a non-instrumental moral will. This will is not just a matter of personal taste because it is conceived as binding for any decent human being. In this way, the structure of Ockham's ethics is intuitively plausible with or without its religious content.

9

Political Theory

So far we have been examining what is known as Ockham's "academic" work. Virtually all of it (filling more than fifteen large recently-
edited tomes) was written while he was a student at Oxford University.
In 1323, just before he would have graduated, Ockham was summoned
to the Papal Court in Avignon to answer to charges of heresy. He was
under investigation for a total of four years and fled before the process
came to completion. This was the end of his academic career. He wrote
a great deal during his twenty years of exile, virtually all of it political
and bearing on his own conflict with Church authority.

Although Ockham's political difficulties began as a dispute over
the orthodoxy of his theology, his conflict with Church authority had
more to do with a controversy concerning the Franciscan Order. A few
generations earlier, Pope Nicholas III had granted the Franciscans permission to follow the example of St. Francis by carrying out their min-
istry in abject poverty. Pope John XXII, however, was now determined
to build a truly decadent castle in the south of France. The incongruity
was becoming embarrassingly obvious: while the Franciscans were
preaching that it was better to be poor like Jesus, the Pope was the rich-
est man in the known world. So, John decided to revoke the permission
to preach in and about abject poverty.

Ockham joined one wing of the Franciscan Order in rebellion
against this decision. He never came to renounce papacy in theory, but
he did become convinced that John XXII and his successors were anti-
popes. In arguing against their actions he developed his own political
theory. It was never as systematic as his academic work, but it was influential. In this chapter we survey some of its most important themes.

9.1 Property

In order to enable the Franciscans to give up all worldly goods, Pope Nicholas III had taken official possession of all Franciscan property: the land they lived on, the clothing they wore, even the very bowls they used for begging when they traveled. Anything you might give to a Franciscan, you were actually giving to the pope, who was de facto allowing the Franciscan to use it as he pleased.

Although this arrangement worked, Pope John XXII refused to uphold it. His motives may have been self-serving, but he had been trained as a lawyer, and he had a good argument. His case rested on two main points: first, it is not clear that the renunciation of ownership has anything at all to do with the Christian ideal of humility; and second, given that the Franciscans had exclusive use of the donations they were given, they, in fact, owned those things. Papal "ownership" was that in name only.

No one was in a better position than a nominalist, however, to show why reducing something to a name is not the same as reducing it to nothing at all. A name, after all, is a mental concept, and a mental concept is an intention. The crux of Ockham's response to John is that the intention to own is altogether different from the intention to use.

Ockham's first task was to consider the concept of ownership. What does it mean to *own* something? In search of an answer, Ockham turns to the experience of freedom that he defended in his libertarian metaphysics. The one thing that human beings can be said to own more than anything else is their free actions. This implies that ownership has to do with sole authorship: we own what we make.

But there are different levels of making. The highest level is creation, exemplified by God's creation of the world. The next level is generation, exemplified when parents generate children. And the last level is production, as when artists produce artifacts. These three levels of making constitute different levels of ownership, and they imply different levels of claim. Since God is the primary owner, he has limitless claim over his creatures. A parent's "ownership" of a child is secondary to God's, so the parent has a claim over the child limited by God's will. Likewise for a child: his ownership of, say, a sandcastle is limited by both his parents and God. To own something is to have an automatic and legitimate claim to do what you will with it consistent with those who have a prior ownership.

This analysis sets the stage for the concept of *use*. To use something is to do as you will with it consistent with the will of its owner. When you borrow a book from the library you may take it where you

84

like and read it, or just look at the pictures, or neither, or both. Yet, this is only because the owner of the book permits these things. You may not rip the book up for use as confetti because the owner forbids it. You are doing as you will with the book just insofar as your will matches the will of the owner.

The reason the Franciscans' use does not amount to ownership, Ockham argues, is that they are only doing as they will with the donations insofar as the owner wills. In usual circumstances the two wills should match in such a way that they are indistinguishable, like seeing white on white. It may occasionally happen, however, that the will of the owner ceases to match the will of the user, and it is in just such a circumstance that the true nature of the user's intention shows itself. When the owner makes his new will known to the user, the user has no claim against it. Ockham put this distinction in terms of *rights*: the owner has a right and the mere user does not.

9.2 Rights

The concept of rights is ubiquitous in contemporary political philosophy, and one of the things that makes pre-modern political philosophy hard to understand is that concept's comparative absence there. The recognition of rights nowadays is far more important than it was in pre-modern days. Some would go so far as identify the birth and growth of the modern liberal state with the birth and growth of personal rights.

There is some controversy as to exactly where and when the concept of rights was invented. It is generally agreed to be absent in ancient Roman law, and fully present in Enlightenment thought. It is difficult to trace the medieval contribution to this development. It has often been noted, however, that the fourteenth-century debate over Franciscan poverty, of all things, was an important turning point.

By putting the distinction between owners and users in terms of rights, Ockham is defining the scope of the law. Having a right to what you use implies that your use is protected by legal authority. If, in contrast, you merely use something recognizing that you have no right to it, then you have no such protection. Renunciation of ownership is renunciation of legal protection. Ockham writes,

> Thus, poor people invited by a rich man have the licit power to use the food and drink put before them, but the inviter can, if he pleases, take them away, and, if he does so, those invited cannot, for this, call the person who invited them into court; they have no action against him. [OPol I 304; K 24]

When the Franciscans insist on being allowed to give up the right of ownership what they are insisting upon is being allowed to give up their right to legal protection. Why would they want to do that? Surely it is always better to have recourse to the law than not.

Ockham disagreed. To avail oneself of legal authority is implicitly to recognize the sovereignty of the state. And it is precisely this that the Franciscans did not want to do. The *raison d'être* of the state is to enforce rights. When the Franciscans renounce ownership what they are renouncing is state authority.

9.3 Anarchy for the Perfect

Ockham's battle against John for the permission to teach in and about abject poverty concerned much more than the ideal of Christian humility. In fact, it was hardly about that at all, since Ockham was not overly critical of wealth, and, as an academic, would have had access to many privileges typically denied to the poor. Rather, what the poverty controversy was about, as far as Ockham was concerned, was the origin and extent of *natural* rights of the individual, and the provision of *artificial* rights, by the state.

Political philosophers often use a *state of nature* thought experiment to illustrate and defend their views on state authority. Ockham's state of nature, as is appropriate in an age that relied so heavily on the religious mode of discourse, is the Garden of Eden. He writes,

> God gave Adam and his wife an ownership common to the whole human race for themselves and all their posterity. It was a power to manage and use temporal things to their own advantage. That power would have gone on existing in the state of innocence without power to appropriate any temporal thing to any one person or to any particular collectivity or to certain persons. Ever since the Fall, however, the common ownership exists together with the power of appropriating temporal things. . . . Once they sinned, avarice and the desire to possess and use temporal things wrongly grew up among humans. So it became useful and expedient that temporal things should be appropriated and not be common any more. The goal was to restrain the immoderate appetite of the wicked for possessing temporal things and to eliminate neglect of the proper management and administration of temporal things. For, common affairs are commonly neglected by bad people. [OPol IV 178-9; M 88-9]

God, as the ultimate owner of everything, gave human beings a license for common ownership of nature. This is basically free use according to need or desire consistent with others' needs and desires. When they began to ignore each other's needs and desires, he gave them a license for individual ownership. It is Ockham's view, then, that human beings have a natural right to create artificial rights. God gives us permission to establish private property and the institutions that support it.

But he does not require it. Ockham is careful in the above quote to say that ever since the Fall "common ownership exists *together with* the power of appropriating temporal things." In fact, it is better to do without private property, if you can. Ockham writes,

> In Matthew 19 Christ says to a young man, "If you wish to be perfect, go, sell all you have, give the money to the poor, and come, and follow me." From these words we gather evidently that Christ taught us to sell riches and give to the poor. When riches are sold and given to the poor, however, they are renounced in respect of lordship and ownership; therefore Christ taught renunciation of the ownership of wealth. [OPol II 695; K103]

This is the central message of the gospel, on Ockham's view. You cannot deny that you are a natural object, and this is why natural rights are inalienable. You can deny that you are a citizen, however. This is, in fact, what Jesus and St. Francis were up to, on Ockham's view.

Ockham's approach to the alienable/inalienable right distinction is unusual. He was not interested in protecting individual rights as inalienable, or in defending the power of the state to remove certain alienable rights. He was interested in alienating *his own right* to hold property. Of course, on a modern view of rights, a right provides a claim that the holder need not exercise; so for example, the right to vote confers no necessity of voting, and the right to property does not mean you are required to own any. Yet, Ockham is making a deeper point. What he wants to say is that life regulated by social institutions is optional and not ideal. The Franciscans wanted to opt out of the state and live in their own apolitical religious community.

9.4 Monarchy for the Fallen

Ockham's political vision rests on the observation that it is both possible and desirable to give up the service that the state offers to its citizens. This is a very different view that of the British philosopher Thomas Hobbes (1588-1679), who stresses the advantages of social institutions, without which life is nasty, brutish, and short. Ockham, in contrast, thinks that individuals can and should leave the state and try to recreate the Garden of Eden. In theory, it would be possible for people to surrender their rights one by one until there was no state left.

But idealistic communal anarchy is not suitable for the vast majority of fallen human beings, who rely on social institutions. If we are going to have a state for those who cannot or will not cooperate voluntarily, what kind should it be?

Ockham is unimpressed with democracy, and has very little to say about it. He does recommend a constitutional form of rule for use within families and societies like the Franciscan order. But for the realm of the Fallen, he favors electing a monarch who rules by will. If he is a great ruler, then they will have an inspiring example. If he is terrible, then they can get rid of him. And if, as is more likely, he is just good enough, then he will enforce the standard needed by those who are unable or unwilling to give up property rights. This is political voluntarism. Ockham writes,

> If in some community all were good and not at all pervertible by wickedness, actual or potential, it would be unjust that someone should rule those similar and equal to himself in wisdom and virtue, because in that case there would seem to be no reason why one should rule rather than another. But when, in some community, there are many or several who have been or can be perverted, and when the greater and more powerful part willingly accepts the rule of one, so that they cannot be diverted from such will, then it is beneficial that one should accept rulership over all, provided a person is found who is worthy to rule over the worse members (since otherwise he could not be regarded as good or suitable). [K 153-4]

A will-based political system simulates the ownership relation that exists naturally between God and creatures, parents and children, artist and artifact.

Ockham is careful not to set too high a standard for the monarch. He points out that the great Old Testament leader Saul was chosen simply because he was tall, literally head and shoulders above the crowd. And he worked out just fine. The main thing is that the monarch must have sufficient human and financial resources to enforce his will. Ockham writes that,

> without riches the imperial office cannot be well administered, for if "jurisdiction without coercion must be counted as nothing," . . . much more is imperial authority nothing without coercion, and coercion cannot be exercised without power.

Therefore, power is required in an emperor. And power seems most of all to be strengthened by riches. [K 280]

People who live in the state want someone to keep track of property, and sheer power is the only way to do that.

In the end, what Ockham has in mind a kind of father figure. For a father you need a good man, not necessarily great, but one who really loves his children, and can punish them—out of this very love—when they are bad. Perhaps Ockham conceives of those who are not ready to leave the state as morally immature, like a child who never quite leaves the nest. So, why not give them what they need? This, at any rate, is the best government to have existing side by side with those who are ready to leave the nest.

The main job of the monarch, besides setting an example, is to establish institutions to protect natural rights against usurpation by others—for those who want such protection. Ockham stresses that since monarchy exists for the common good, it should be open to input and correction. He tries to provide some direction as to how such a limited monarchy should work, but it is clear that his heart is not in it. After all, the state is (or, at least, should be) only very indirectly relevant to Franciscan existence.

Ockham lived out his exile in Munich under the protection of Louis of Bavaria, the self-styled, and unconsecrated, "Holy Roman Emperor." There is an old legend according to which Ockham, upon meeting Louis, said to him: "Sire, defend me with your sword, and I shall defend you with my pen." Ockham almost certainly said no such thing. If anyone were liable to have bartered pen for sword, it would have been Ockham's contemporary, Marsilius of Padua (1275-1343). Marsilius was forced to seek protection in Munich at the same time as Ockham due to the publication of his anti-papal treatise, *The Defender of the Peace*, which he dedicated to "the most exalted Louis."

Marsilius's position represents the third leg of the political triangle that drove the fourteenth century. Three competing political visions had emerged. First, there was "hierocracy," according to which the pope is the highest ruler in the land with a "plenitude of power" even to make and break monarchs. Second, there was "imperialism," according to which the pope is an appointee of the state. Finally, there was "separatism," which cast pope and monarch as independent powers in separate spheres. Simply put, Pope John and his supporters were pushing for the first, Marsilius and Louis were pushing for the second, and Ockham was pushing for the third.

9.5 Separation of Church and State

Today when we think of separation of church and state we think of getting religion out of public institutions. Ockham devoted a lot of energy toward separatism, but his concern was the reverse: to get public institutions out of religion.

Ockham argues that John XXII and the two popes who followed him were covert politicos and only pretenders to the papacy. His whole argument is based on the claim that they were introducing secular matters (like property) into the spiritual realm and thereby destroying the distinct character of the spiritual community.

The pope is one of the apostles. His job is to be a spiritual authority: teaching morality by his own example, reminding us when we stray, and reprimanding us when we refuse to come back. This should be sufficient leadership for those who are striving to be perfect.

So, what is the distinct character of the spiritual community according to Ockham? It consists in the categorical rejection of the central prerogative of secular authority: coercion. Coercive authority, of course, operates by the threat of physical punishment. Yet, this is something unsuitable to the spiritual realm, according to Ockham. He writes,

> For this reason, the head of Christians does not, as a rule, have power to punish secular wrongs with a capital penalty and other bodily penalties and it is for thus punishing such wrongs that temporal power and riches are chiefly necessary; such punishment is granted chiefly to the secular power. The pope, therefore, can, as a rule, correct wrongdoers only with a spiritual penalty. It is not, therefore, necessary that he should excel in temporal power or abound in temporal riches, but it is enough that Christians should willingly obey him. [K 204]

Hence, there can be no argument, as John was want to make, that clergymen and the pope, in particular, need to own wealth. They can and should go without ownership, if they want to be examples of the true faith. (This, of course, raises the question of who would own the goods the Franciscans were using if not the pope. A good emperor, no doubt, could handle that job equally well.)

So Ockham paints a picture of church and state existing side by side, the latter with life-and-death coercive power, the former with no power of physical punishment at all. This was almost unimaginable in his day. But notice that it is the very picture that eventually won out.

9.6 Ockham Against Representation

People often herald Ockham as a forerunner of Protestantism. There are some obvious connections, but there are also important differences. For one thing, the rise of Protestantism is often associated with the opposition to hierarchical governance, and the advocacy instead of representational governing institutions, in both the secular and ecclesiastical realms. Ockham, however, was very anti-representationalist in his conception of leadership.

It follows directly from his nominalism that, strictly speaking, political unities do not exist, so there is no such thing as a common, universal, or "general" will for a political representative to represent. All that exists is individual wills, and people who accept formal representation are submitting their wills to that of someone else.

Medieval "organicists" took the metaphor of political association as "body" very seriously. They went so far as to grant such bodies the status of persons. In opposition to this, Ockham writes,

> If the order of the Friars Minor is a person represented and imaginary, then by the same reason the church and all other communities would be persons represented and imaginary. And this is absurd. For, what is only represented and imaginary is fantastical, and is not in things outside the mind. [OPol II 568]

Ockham does not object to limited forms of representation like delegation and council as long as their objectives are specific and clear.

9.7 Freedom of Speech

Ockham was deeply interested in freedom of speech. This is not surprising considering that his own political involvement started with accusations of heresy in his philosophy. Of course, heresy is an all but forgotten concept in modern political philosophy, except in so far as it is the forerunner of modern problems involving speech restriction.

According to Aquinas's political theory, a heretic only had three chances to repent before he was turned over to the secular authorities for execution. Ockham was very strongly opposed to this. In his political dialogue, he writes:

> Student: What if someone were to defend heresy that she said she thought was consonant with the orthodox faith in front of the pope?

> Teacher: They say that if she were to defend heresy a thousand times unknowingly with the express or implicit protestation that she is prepared to be corrected as soon as she recognizes her opinions to contradict the Catholic faith, then she should not be judged a heretic, especially in front of the pope. [Dial 457]

Ockham's argument for free speech rests on the assumption that it is up to every individual to decide for herself what is worthy of belief, and to try to correct her community if she thinks that it errs.

The key to Ockham's understanding of Church authority in this regard lies in his use of Jesus' promise to his disciples that he would "be with them always, to the end of the age." [Matthew 28:20] A popular medieval interpretation of this promise was that the Catholic Church, as represented by the pope, could never err, that is, that it is impossible for the church to institutionalize error. If *ex cathedra* pronouncements are infallible, there should be no need for the church to leave its official, time-tested truths open to correction.

On Ockham's view, in contrast, it *is* possible for the church to institutionalize error. He argues that the minimum required for Jesus to fulfill his promise is that at least one individual remain faithful at any given time. Nor is this person's faith necessarily identifiable with official church doctrine. On the contrary, Ockham develops a long and intense argument culminating in the conclusion that the entire faith community could be preserved in a single baptized infant. "Infants have the disposition of faith," he writes, "Therefore, if the whole multitude of Christians having use of reason erred, it would be possible to preserve the promise of Christ through baptized infants." [Dial 504]

This use of Ockham's razor leaves us with very little institution, and hence very little official church doctrine that is not open to correction. Suppose that the totality of true believers actually was reduced to a single infant and that she grew up amidst heretics, never accepting their heresy, nor publicly protesting it for some good reason. We can imagine a faith community surviving underground in this way for generation upon generation. In fact, preserving his disciples in secret while the rest of the world has gone to hell would be one very plausible way for God to fulfill his promise to be with them always and forever.

After angrily describing the spiritual chaos that rampant heresy, war, and property mongering has caused throughout Christendom, Ockham asserts that Christians should not be so sure that things can only get better. He writes,

> Some say that during the time of the Antichrist there will be such a persecution and extinction of Catholics that every region in the entire world will be occupied by infidels or apostates. And they say that it is not possible to know through the divine scriptures or the doctrine of the universal church whether something similar will or will not happen *before* the time of the Antichrist. [Dial 503]

So how do we know that this apocalyptic scenario has not taken place? The only solution is to judge for oneself whether or not the church has institutionalized error. This analysis would seem to apply to the teachings of the saints, the record of sacred history, and the Bible itself, since any of these things might conceivably have been made official while the true believers were powerless to prevent it.

Of course, Ockham's view that God can do anything that is logically possible directly implies that God can break any promise he pleases. This always remains true even though God in fact never does break any of his promises. The point of Ockham's apocalyptic scenario is to show that God could allow all of Christendom (save one) to run afoul without even breaking any promises.

Ockham assures us that this has not in fact happened; all of the time-tested doctrines of the church are indeed true, at least, if interpreted in the right way. Not only that, but he grants that a true pope has the authority to prohibit Catholics from making assertions deliberately designed to undermine the Faith. His concern is to show that this authority is not infallible.

He is also concerned to show that this authority is strictly limited to the theological sphere. No one, whether pope, monarch, or university official has the authority to prohibit non-theological assertions. Ockham writes,

> Assertions, especially in physics, that do not pertain to theology should not be officially condemned or prohibited by anyone, because in such things everyone should be free so that they may freely say what they please. [Dial 425]

9.8 Ockham's Legacy

Ockham does not often explicitly try to connect his political theory to his earlier work in metaphysics, epistemology, or even ethics. He was addressing a different audience now, one that would not necessarily have been familiar with the university debates. Nevertheless, there are clear connections, and we have been able to survey a few. His eliminativist methodology enables him to demystify political entities, his voluntarism makes him partial to personal as opposed to institutional rule, and his libertarianism provides a basis for defending natural rights. As elsewhere in his philosophy, these ideas add up to a major turning point: the beginnings of modernity. In political terms, this consists in the breakdown of the organic social and political ideals, and the rise of individualism.

Ockham's political works were condemned, but this did not prevent them from circulating widely underground. So many unauthorized copies of his political dialogue were produced that it has been almost impossible to put together a critical edition. (It is still in progress.) Ockham's academic works were not condemned, but they remain unfinished and hardly received the attention they deserved. In fact, various academics throughout Europe got into serious trouble with university authorities for pursuing nominalism in the years after Ockham's death. It is no wonder that Ockham is a rather obscure figure in the history of philosophy, considering how long his work was officially considered anathema.

Ockham was a passionate man and an original thinker, notorious in his own time for his fearless intelligence. He was a worthy adversary of one of the most powerful popes in the history of the papacy. John XXII once announced that he was prepared to burn a town down to smoke Ockham out. But he could not put an end to Ockham, nor to Ockhamism, and the growing awareness that it was time for change.

Bibliography

All of Ockham's works were originally written in Latin, almost all of them have been expertly edited, and several have been translated. Most of the quoted passages in this book are original translations by Kaye, though she has consulted any known translations. The abbreviations we use in citations refer to the list of works below:

[OPh, OTh] William of Ockham, *Opera Philosophica et Theologica (Philosophical and Theological Works)*, G. Gál et al. eds., NY: The Franciscan Institute, 1967-88, 17 vols. This is the definitive edition of all of Ockham's surviving non-political works. Seven of these volumes are designated *Opera Philosophica*, which we abbreviate **[OPh]**, and the remaining ten, *Opera Theologica*, which we abbreviate **[OTh]**. A volume number and a page number follow these abbreviations.

Translations of Selected Parts of [OPh]:

[A] Adams, Marilyn McCord and Norman Kretzmann, trs., *Predestination, God's Foreknowledge, and Future Contingents*, Indianapolis: Hackett, 1983.

[B] Boehner, Philotheus, O.F.M., tr., *Ockham: Philosophical Writings, A Selection*, Indianapolis: Hackett, 1990.

[L] Loux, Michael J., tr., *Ockham's Theory of Terms: Part One of the Summa Logicae*, Notre Dame: University of Notre Dame Press, 1974.

[F] Freddoso, Alfred J. and Henry Schuurman, trs., *Ockham's Theory of Propositions: Part II of the Summa Logicae*, Notre Dame: University of Notre Dame Press, 1980.

Translations of Selected Parts of [OTh]:

[Q] Freddoso, Alfred J. and Francis E. Kelly, trs., *Quodlibetal Questions*, New Haven: Yale University Press, 1991. A citation like **[Quod 7.1]** refers to a standard section found in **[Q]** and the original **[OTh IX]**.

[W] Wood, Rega, tr., *Ockham on the Virtues*, West Lafayette: Purdue University Press, 1997.

[OPol] William of Ockham, *Opera Politica (Political Works)*, H. S. Offler et al. eds., Manchester: The University Press, 1956-74, vols. I-III; Oxford: Oxford University Press, 1997, vol. IV. This edition contains all of Ockham's political works except the *Dialogus*.

[Dial] William of Ockham, *Dialogus*, Melchior Goldast ed., Torino: Bottega d'Erasmo, 1959. See also the internet edition, in progress, by John Kilcullen et al:
http://britac3.britac.ac.uk/pubs/dialogus/ockdial.html.

Translations of Selected Political Texts:

[K] McGrade, A. S. and John Kilcullen, trs., *A Letter to the Friars Minor and Other Writings*, Cambridge: Cambridge University Press, 1995.

[M] McGrade, A. S. and John Kilcullen, trs., *A Short Discourse on Tyrannical Government*, Cambridge: Cambridge University Press, 1992.

Other Authors Cited:

[T] Thomas Aquinas, *Quaestiones disputatae*, vol. II, pt. 1, ed. R. Spiazzi, Taurini, Romae: Marietti, 1953.

[J] John Duns Scotus, *Opera Omnia*, vol. VII, ed., P.C. Balić, Vatican: Typis Polyglottis Vaticanis, 1973.

Secondary Sources for Further Reference:

Adams, Marilyn McCord, *William Ockham*, Notre Dame: University of Notre Dame Press, 1987.

Goddu, André, *The Physics of William of Ockham*, Leiden: E.J. Brill, 1984.

McGrade, A.S., *The Political Thought of William of Ockham: Personal and Institutional Principles*, Cambridge: Cambridge University Press, 1974.

Spade, Paul, *The Cambridge Companion to Ockham*, Cambridge: Cambridge University Press, 1999.